301
Country
Christmas
Quilt Blocks

301
Country Christmas
Quilt Blocks

Cheri Saffiote

Sterling Publishing Co., Inc. New York
A Sterling/Chapelle Book

Chapelle, Ltd.

Owner: Jo Packham

Editor: Karmen Quinney

Staff: Areta Bingham, Kass Burchett, Ray Cornia, Marilyn Goff, Karla Haberstich, Holly Hollingsworth, Susan Jorgensen, Barbara Milburn, Caroll Shreeve, Cindy Stoeckl, Kim Taylor, Sara Toliver, Desirée Wybrow

Artwork: Shauna Kawasaki

Photo Stylist: Jill Dahlberg

Photography: Kevin Dilley for Hazen Photography

CREATE IT
Present

Techniques: Pieced, Appliquéd

Library of Congress Cataloging-in-Publication Data

Saffiote, Cheri.
    301 country Christmas quilt blocks / Cheri Saffiote.
       p. cm.
    "A Sterling/Chapelle book."
    ISBN 0-8069-8275-6
      1. Quilting—Patterns. 2. Patchwork—Patterns. 3. Appliqué—Patterns
    4. Christmas decorations. I. Title: Three hundred one country Christmas
    quilt blocks. II. Title: Three hundred and one country Christmas quilt blocks.
    III. Title.

    TT835.S23 2002
    746.46'041—dc21   2002021696
    10 9 8 7 6 5 4 3 2 1

A Sterling/Chapelle Book

Published by Sterling Publishing Co., Inc.
387 Park Avenue South, New York, NY 10016
© 2002 by Cheri Saffiote
Distributed in Canada by Sterling Publishing
℅ Canadian Manda Group, One Atlantic Avenue, Suite 105
Toronto, Ontario, Canada M6K 3E7
Distributed in Australia by Capricorn Link (Australia) Pty. Ltd.
P.O. Box 704, Windsor, NSW 2756, Australia
Printed in USA

Sterling ISBN 0-8069-8275-6

Every effort has been made to ensure that all of the information in this book is accurate. However, due to differing conditions, tools, and individual skills, the publisher cannot be responsible for any injuries, losses, and/or any other damages which may result from the use of the information in this book.

Due to the limited amount of space available, we must print our patterns at a reduced size in order to give our patrons the maximum number of patterns possible in our publications. We believe the quality and quantity of our patterns will compensate for any inconvenience this may cause.

If you have any questions or comments, please contact:

Chapelle, Ltd., Inc.
P.O. Box 9252
Ogden, UT 84409
Phone: (801) 621-2777
FAX: (801) 621-2788
e-mail: chapelle@chapelleltd.com
website: www.chapelleltd.com

Contents

Introduction

The 301 Christmas quilt blocks featured in this book were made from 100% cotton fabric and wool felt. Fabric scraps or 1/4 yd fabric pieces are recommended. When selecting fabrics to use on your quilts, imagine what that motif would look like if it were real. A tree is not all one shade of green, so it would make sense to select several shades of green to use in making a tree. Try making the bottom of the tree darker, then gradually making it lighter at the top. You may want one side of the tree to have more shadow; therefore, it would be darker on that side. Lay out the fabrics in a shape similar to the finished piece to see if they give you the look you are seeking.

The finished quilts featured in this book are created to look as though they were made from fabrics found in grandma's attic, and the colors have darkened with time. The fabrics used were tea-dyed to achieve that look.

Quilt blocks labeled "**CREATE IT**" are simply ideas for the endless possibilities of creating Christmas quilt blocks.

Types of Quilt Blocks

The quilt blocks in this book were created using the following four techniques or a combination of these techniques: appliquéd, embroidered, pieced, and template pieced.

Appliquéd Quilt Block

Embroidered Quilt Block

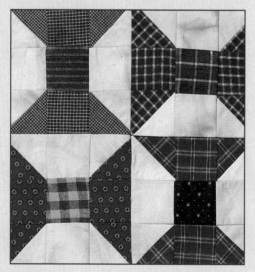

Pieced Quilt Block

Template-pieced Quilt Block

Quilt Block Patterns

Photocopy patterns from book or trace over patterns with a pencil and tracing paper. Enlarge all patterns on photocopier at 200% unless otherwise indicated. Using craft scissors, cut out patterns.

The number after the pattern tells how many motifs from each pattern are needed. For example, you will need to cut five motifs from the Golden Ring pattern below.

Golden Ring (5)

Appliquéd Quilt Blocks

Appliqué pieces are used to highlight and/or add detail to a background block. Appliqués can be cut from all types of fabrics. Heavy fabrics such as felt or wool add more dimension to a quilt block. They can be detailed with a variety of stitches. Embellishments such as buttons and charms can be added to appliquéd pieces. Appliqués can be fused onto a background block if desired.

Instructions for Appliqué Technique

1. Using permanent marker, trace pattern onto paper side of freezer paper for template.
2. Using craft scissors, cut out template.
3. With doubled fabric, right sides together, iron template with waxed side down onto fabric.
4. Stitch completely around template. Backstitch at end.
5. Using fabric scissors, cut around template 1/8" from stitching line. Peel off paper.
   Note: Freezer paper templates are reusable.
6. Trim any tight curves.
7. Make a slit on back side of motif, turn right side out, and press.
8. Position motif on background block.
9. Hand-stitch motif in place.

Instructions for Fused-appliqué Technique

1. Trace reverse pattern onto paper side of double-sided fusible web. The outline will be a mirror image of the motif. Using craft scissors, cut out web motif, allowing a small margin.
2. Iron adhesive side of motif onto wrong side of appliqué fabric, following manufacturer's instructions. Using fabric scissors, cut out motif.
3. Peel off and discard paper backing. Iron motif onto background block.

Embroidered Quilt Blocks

When creating an embroidered quilt block, it will be necessary to transfer the pattern onto the background fabric. There are three basic transferring methods available: freehand, tracing paper, and tear-away stabilizer.

Transferring Methods

Freehand
Using a fabric marker, draw design onto fabric.

Tracing Paper
Trace design onto tracing paper. Turn paper over. Using iron-on transfer pencil, trace over lines on reverse side of paper. Place tracing paper with transfer pencil side down on fabric. Iron. Note: This is a permanent line that will need to be covered.

Tear-away Stabilizer
Trace pattern onto stabilizer. Baste-stitch or pin stabilizer to fabric. Stitch pattern through stabilizer. When complete, tear away stabilizer and discard.

Instructions for Embroidered Technique

1. Complete background block as desired.
2. Using desired transferring method, transfer design onto fabric.
3. Using appropriate stitches, embroider design.

Pieced Quilt Blocks

Fabric shapes such as squares, triangles, and rectangles are used to create traditional quilt blocks.

Instructions for Pieced Technique

1. Cut out all fabric pieces as indicated on project's quilt diagram. All measurements given include $1/4$" seam allowances.
2. Make certain to lay out fabric pieces to determine placement before beginning the sewing process.
3. Stitch pieces as shown in project. Work from the center out unless otherwise indicated.

Pieced Quilt Block Legend

The following symbols will be used for pieced quilt block instructions:

 Cut square in half diagonally.

 Cut square in half diagonally twice.

 Lay two squares of coordinating fabrics, right sides together. Sew all four sides with $1/4$" seam allowance. Iron. Cut in half diagonally twice. Open triangles into squares and iron.

Snowballing Corners

 Lay small square on corner of larger square with right sides together, even with top and side edges. Sew diagonally across small square.

 Trim off corner to $1/4$" from seam. Fold reminder of small square over seam and iron.

 Repeat for all four corners.

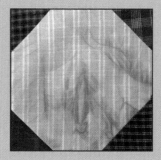

Snowball-cornered Quilt Block

Template-pieced Quilt Blocks

Template-pieced sections vary in size and shape, yet together they form a unique quilt block. These quilt blocks are geometrical but not symmetrical. Appliqués can be whipstitched or fused onto a background block if desired. Embroidery can also be added.

Instructions for Template-pieced Technique

1. Using permanent marker, trace pattern onto paper side of freezer paper for template.
2. Using craft scissors, cut out template, adding $1/4$" seam allowances.
3. Iron template with waxed side down onto right side of fabric.
   Note: If multiple designs are needed, layer fabric with right sides up and cut as one.
4. Using fabric scissors, cut around template.
   Note: A rotary cutter can be used if desired.
5. Peel template from fabric.
   Note: Freezer paper templates are reusable.
6. Stitch pieces into strips, following numerical sequence.
7. Stitch strips together to assemble.

Log Cabin Strips

When creating log cabin strips, the only pieces that must be cut precisely are the center block and the background block. All strips must be uniform only in width; the length will be trimmed at sewing time. The combination of light and dark strips establishes the look of the log cabin. Log cabin strips make a great pattern to use up scraps of fabrics.

Instructions for Log Cabin Strips

1. Find centers of background block and the center block. Mark. Baste center of center block to center of background block.

2. Cut strips for logs. Place one on center block, right sides together, matching top raw edges. Stitch seam.

3. Trim bottom edge even with center block. Press open.

4. Continue adding log cabin strips around block, sewing and trimming until block reaches desired size.

Note: Add log cabin strips in a counterclockwise rotation, alternating light and dark strips, until desired size and look are achieved.

Appliquéd Quilt Block with Log Cabin Strips

Finishing

Instructions for Finishing

1. Cut backing larger than quilt top.

2. Lay batting on wrong side of backing.

3. Lay quilt top on batting, right side up. Smooth out any wrinkles. Pin or baste into place.

4. Quilt as desired.

5. Trim back and batting to same size as top.

Binding

Instructions for Binding

1. Cut binding strips to desired width.

2. Line up edges with right sides together at front of quilt. Stitch edge of binding to outside edge of quilt.

3. Fold remaining edge of binding over ¼", then fold binding over edge of quilt. Blind-stitch or machine-stitch binding in place on back of quilt.

Tea-dyed Fabric

All types of fabrics can be tea-dyed, but muslin is most commonly used. When applying tea dye to fabrics, do not put light-colored fabrics and dark-colored fabrics together.

Instructions for Tea-dyed Fabric

1. Place one jar instant tea and approximately six tablespoons instant coffee into large kettle filled with water.

2. Heat over medium temperature until mixture is hot, but not boiling. Remove from heat.

3. Immerse fabric in tea-dye mixture to soak for at least 30 minutes. When fabric has been dyed to desired color, remove from mixture and wring out. When possible, hang fabric outside to air-dry; this will make the dye darker.

To tea-dye an entire quilt block once it has been completed, place the tea-dye mixture into a spray bottle, spray the project in a sink or dish to avoid overspray. Allow fabric to air-dry.

Tea-dyed Quilt Block

Primitive Stitches

Backstitch

1. Insert needle up through fabric at A, using three strands of floss.

2. Go down at B, one stitch length to the right.

3. Come up at C, one stitch length to left.

4. Go down at A.

Baste Stitch

1. Insert needle up through fabric at A, using three strands of floss.
2. Go down at B, creating a line of straight stitches with an unstitched area between each stitch.
3. Come up at C. Repeat.

Blind Stitch

Note: Blind stitches are used to attach the binding to the back of the quilt.

1. Insert needle up at A, using three strands of floss.
2. Cross diagonally on lower fabric, taking a small horizontal stitch at B.
3. Come up at C. Cross diagonally back to upper fabric, keeping horizontal stitches small on reverse side of fabric. Repeat.

Buttonhole Stitch

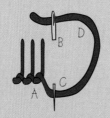

1. Insert needle up through fabric at A, using three strands of floss.
2. Go down at B.
3. Come up at C, keeping floss under needle.
4. Go down at D. Repeat.

French Knot

1. Insert needle up through fabric at A, using three strands of floss.
2. Loosely wrap floss once around needle.
3. Go down at B, next to A. Pull floss taut as needle is pushed down through fabric.
4. Carry floss across back of work between knots.

Feather Stitch

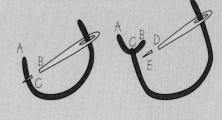

1. Insert needle up through fabric at A, using three strands of floss.
2. Go down at B.
3. Come up at C, keeping floss under the needle, holding it in a "V" shape. Pull floss flat.
4. Go down at D.
5. Come up at E. Repeat.

Whipstitch

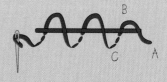

1. Insert needle up through both layers of fabric at A, using three strands of floss.
2. Go down at B through single layer of fabric. Pass needle between layers over to C.
3. Come up at C through both layers of fabric. Repeat.

CREATE IT

CREATE IT
Camel

Techniques: Template Pieced, Appliquéd, Embroidered

Countdown to Christmas...

... Chapter 1

CREATE IT

CREATE IT

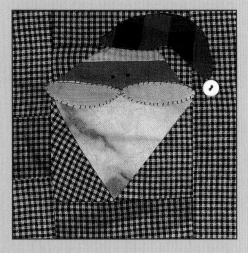

CREATE IT

Christmas Quilt Sampler (21½" x 31½")

Technique: Pieced

Materials & Tools

Backing fabric (1 yd)
Coordinating thread
Cotton fabrics: burgundy plaid (2 yds); green plaid (½ yd)
Fabric scissors
Iron/ironing board
Muslin fabric (1 yd)
Quilt batting
Sewing machine
Sewing needle
Tape measure

Instructions

1. Using dimensions shown in Diagrams A–F cut pieces from desired fabrics.

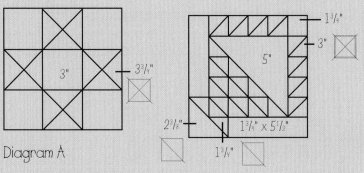

Diagram A

Diagram B

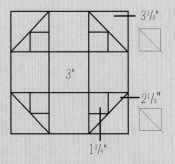

Diagram C

Diagram D

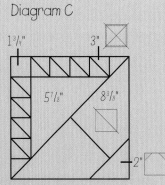

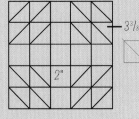

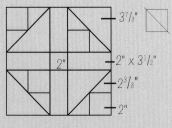

Diagram E

Diagram F

12

2. Stitch pieces together as shown in photo on page 11 for blocks A–F.

3. Using ½" bias tape for stem, whipstitch motif in place as shown in photo below.

4. Cut fourteen 1½" x 8" strips from muslin.

5. Cut seven 1¼" x 8" strips from burgundy plaid fabric.

6. Cut six 3¼" squares from burgundy plaid fabric.

7. Stitch two muslin strips to each long side of a burgundy plaid strip, creating inside border.

8. Repeat Step 7 six times.

9. Stitch block A to top of one inside border.

10. Repeat for blocks B, C, and D.

11. Stitch bottom of block A to top of block C. Stitch bottom of block C to top of block E.

12. Repeat Step 11 for blocks B, D, and F.

13. Stitch two 3¼" squares between remaining inside borders, running end to end as shown in Diagram G for center border.

Diagram G

14. Stitch one long edge of each block strip to each long edge of center border as shown in photo.

15. Cut two 1½" x 17¼" strips from muslin. Cut two 1¼" x 17¼" strips from burgundy plaid fabric .

16. Stitch one muslin strip to each long side of a burgundy plaid strips for top and bottom borders.

17. Cut four 1½" x 26¼" strips from muslin. Cut two 1¼" x 26¼" strips from burgundy plaid fabric.

18. Repeat Step 16 for outside borders.

19. Stitch one 3¼" square from burgundy plaid fabric to each end of top and bottom borders.

20. Stitch one outside border to each side of quilt front. Stitch top and bottom borders to quilt front.

21. Cut batting slightly larger than quilt front.

22. Cut backing fabric to size of quilt front.

23. Place quilt front on batting and place both on wrong side of backing. Baste layers together. Quilt layers.

24. Cut two 1" x 31½" strips and two 1" x 22" strips from burgundy plaid fabric for binding.

25. Stitch one short strip to top and bottom of quilt front for binding. Stitch one long strip to each side of quilt front. Fold and press seam allowance of binding. Fold binding over edge of quilt.

26. Blind-stich binding to back of quilt.

Partridge in a Pear Tree (9" x 11")

Techniques: Appliquéd, Embroidered

1. Prepare and assemble patterns on page 116. Whipstitch motifs in place as shown in photo at left.

2. Stitch button in place as shown.

3. Embroider stems as shown.

Two Turtledoves (8½" x 11¾")

Technique: Appliquéd

1. Prepare and assemble patterns on page 116.

2. Whipstitch motifs in place as shown in photo at right.

Three French Hens (8" x 4½")

Technique: Embroidered

1. Prepare and transfer patterns on page 116 onto background fabric.

2. Embroider designs as shown.

Four Calling Birds

(8" x 8")

Technique: Pieced

1. Using dimensions shown in Diagram A, cut pieces from desired fabrics.

2. Stitch pieces together as shown in photo at left.

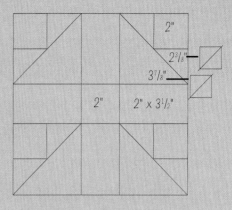

Diagram A

Five Golden Rings

(9¼" x 5¼")

Techniques: Pieced, Appliquéd, Embroidered

1. Using dimensions shown in Diagram B, cut pieces from desired fabrics.

2. Prepare and assemble patterns below. Whipstitch motifs in place on background fabric as shown in photo at right.

3. Embroider design as shown in placement below.

4. Stitch pieces together as shown in photo.

Golden Ring Pattern (5) Actual Size

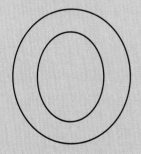

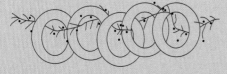

Embroidery Placement

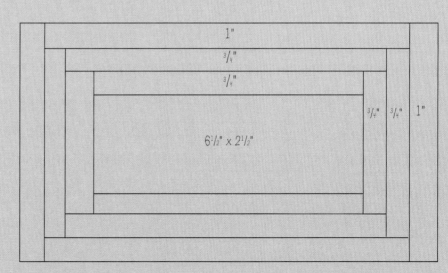

Diagram B

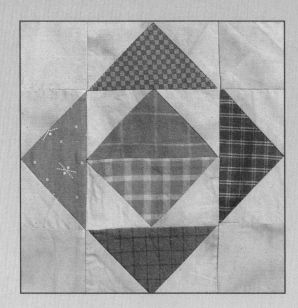

Six Geese-a-Laying

(8½" x 8½")

Technique: Pieced

1. Using dimensions shown in Diagram A, cut pieces from desired fabrics.

2. Stitch pieces together as shown in photo at left.

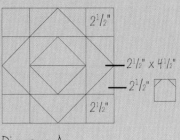

2½"

2½" x 4½"

2½"

2½"

Diagram A

Seven Swans-a-Swimming

(8¼" x 8¼")

Technique: Pieced

1. Using dimensions shown in Diagram B, cut pieces from desired fabrics.

2. Stitch pieces together as shown in photo at right.

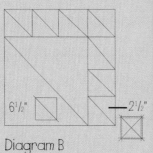

6½"

2½"

Diagram B

Eight Maids-a-Milking (7" x 7½")

Techniques: Template Pieced, Appliquéd, Embroidered

1. Prepare and assemble template on page 117. Stitch pieces into strips, following numerical sequence.

2. Assemble block by stitching strips together.

3. Prepare and assemble patterns on page 117. Whipstitch motifs in place as shown in photo at left.

4. Stitch button in place as shown.

5. Embroider eyes and cheeks as shown.

Nine Ladies Dancing (7" x 11½")

Techniques: Appliquéd, Embroidered

1. Prepare and assemble patterns on page 117. Whipstitch motifs in place as shown in photo at left.

2. Embroider design as shown in placement below.

3. Stitch button in place as shown in photo.

4. Embroider eyes as shown.

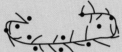

Embroidery Placement

Ten Drummers Drumming (6½" x 7")

Techniques: Template Pieced, Appliquéd, Embroidered

1. Prepare and assemble template on page 117. Stitch pieces into strips, following numerical sequence.

2. Assemble block by stitching strips together.

3. Prepare pattern below. Whipstitch motif in place as shown in photo at right.

4. Embroider eyes and drumsticks as shown.

Hat Décor Pattern

Eleven Lords-a-Leaping (8" x 7½")

Techniques: Appliquéd, Embroidered

1. Prepare and assemble patterns on page 117. Whipstitch motifs in place as shown in photo at left.

2. Embroider eyes and buttons as shown.

CREATE IT
Jack-in-the-Box

Techniques: Pieced, Appliquéd, Embroidered

Twelve Pipers Piping (4" x 8½")

Techniques: Appliquéd, Embroidered

1. Prepare and assemble patterns on page 116. Whipstitch motifs in place as shown in photo at right, except hat.

2. Embroider eyes, mouth, buttons, and hair as shown.

3. Whipstitch hat in place as shown.

Jingle Bells . . .

. . . Chapter 2

Folk-art Poinsettia Basket Runner

(39¼" x 13½")
Techniques: Pieced, Appliquéd

Materials & Tools

Backing fabric (½ yd)
Coordinating thread
Cotton fabrics: green, 4 assorted; prints, 3"-square scraps
Fabric scissors
Felts: burgundy; green; yellow
Flannel: burgundy plaid (½ yd)
Iron/ironing board
Quilt batting
Sewing machine
Sewing needle
Tape measure

Instructions

1. Using dimensions shown in Diagram A, cut pieces from desired fabrics.

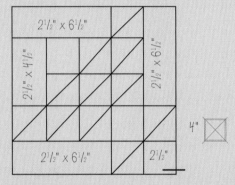

2½" x 6½"
2½" x 4½"
2½" x 6½"
2½" x 6½"
2½" x 6½"
2½"
4"

Diagram A

2. Stitch pieces together as shown in photo at left. Repeat two times.

3. Cut six 8" squares from desired green fabrics. Cut each square in half diagonally. Stitch one triangle onto each side of each block. as shown in Diagram B.

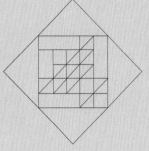

Diagram B

4. Prepare and assemble patterns on page 118. Whipstitch motifs in place as shown in photo below.

5. Stitch three quilt blocks together horizontally in a strip, alternating pattern directions.

6. Cut twelve 3" squares from desired fabrics. Fold and press each square in half, wrong sides together. Fold and press in half again, creating prairie points.

7. Baste six prairie points to each end of strip for runner front, laying points inward and overlapping ends of the points.

8. Cut batting to size of runner front.

9. Cut backing fabric to size of runner front.

10. Place runner front on batting and place both on wrong side of backing. Baste layers together. Quilt layers diagonally. Avoid quilting over appliqués.

11. Cut two 1" x 13½" and two 1" x 39¼" strips from backing fabric for binding.

12. Stitch one long strip to top and bottom of runner front for binding. Stitch one strip to each side of runner front. Fold and press seam allowance of binding. Fold binding over edges of runner.

13. Blind-stitch binding to back of runner.

Angel Chorus (12" x 8¼")

Techniques: Template Pieced, Appliquéd

1. Prepare and assemble template on page 118. Stitch pieces into strips, following numerical sequence.

2. Assemble blocks by stitching strips together.

3. Repeat Steps 1–2 two times.

4. Stitch three blocks together as shown in photo at left.

5. Prepare and assemble patterns on page 118. Whipstitch motifs in place as shown in photo.

Father Christmas (6" x 8½")

Technique: Appliquéd

1. Prepare and assemble patterns on page 118.

2. Whipstitch motifs in place as shown in photo above.

Plain Snowman (4½" x 8")

Techniques: Appliquéd, Embroidered

1. Prepare and assemble patterns on page 158. Whipstitch motifs in place as shown in photo above.

2. Embroider buttons as shown.

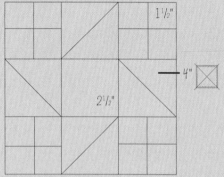

Diagram A

Checkerboard Star (6" x 6")

Technique: Pieced

1. Using dimensions shown in Diagram A, cut pieces from desired fabrics.

2. Stitch pieces together as shown in photo above.

Chili Pepper (4" x 4¾")

Technique: Template Pieced

1. Prepare and assemble template on page 121. Stitch pieces into strips, following numerical sequence.

2. Assemble block by stitching strips together.

Fat Tree

(8½" x 8¼")

Technique: Pieced

1. Using dimensions shown in Diagram B, cut pieces from desired fabrics.

2. Stitch pieces together as shown in photo at left.

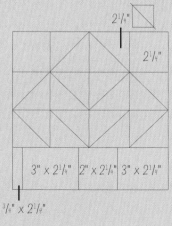

Diagram B

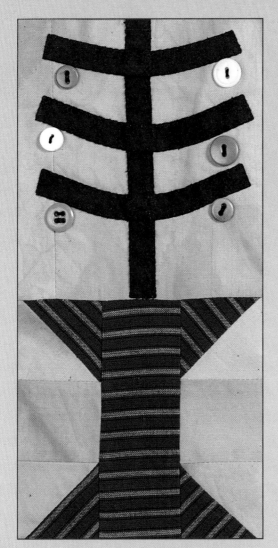

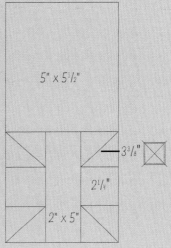

5" × 5½"

3⅜"

2¼"

2" × 5"

Diagram A

Button Tree (5" × 10")

Techniques: Pieced, Appliquéd

1. Using dimensions shown in Diagram A, cut pieces from desired fabrics. Stitch pieces together as shown in photo at left.

2. Prepare and assemble patterns on page 121. Whipstitch motifs in place as shown in photo.

3. Stitch buttons in place as shown.

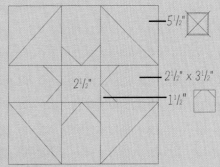

5½"

2½" × 3½"

2½"

1½"

Diagram B

Star Wreath (8¼" × 8¼")

Technique: Pieced

1. Using dimensions shown in Diagram B, cut pieces from desired fabrics.

2. Stitch pieces together as shown in photo at left.

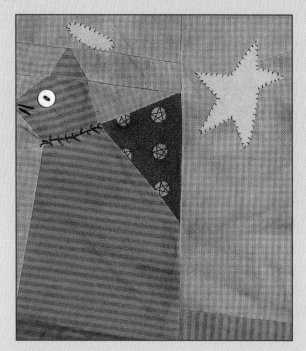

Angel with Harp (4½" x 8½")

Techniques: Template Pieced, Appliquéd

1. Prepare and assemble template on page 121. Stitch pieces into strips, following numerical sequence.

2. Assemble block by stitching strips together.

3. Prepare and assemble patterns on page 121. Whipstitch motifs in place as shown in photo below.

Cat Angel (7" x 7½")

Techniques: Template Pieced, Appliquéd, Embroidered

1. Prepare and assemble template on page 120. Stitch pieces into strips, following numerical sequence.

2. Assemble block by stitching strips together.

3. Prepare and assemble patterns on page 120. Whipstitch motifs in place as shown in photo above.

4. Embroider designs as shown in placements below.

5. Stitch button in place as shown in photo.

Embroidery Placements

Dashing Through the Snow

(8½" x 6½")

Techniques: Appliquéd, Embroidered

1. Prepare and assemble patterns on page 121. Whipstitch motifs in place as shown in photo at left.

2. Embroider eyes as shown.

This pillow was created using the Holly Time quilt block on page 26.

Holly Time (12" x 12")

Techniques: Pieced, Appliquéd

1. Using dimensions shown in Diagram A, cut pieces from desired fabrics. Stitch pieces together as shown in photo above.

2. Prepare and assemble patterns below. Whipstitch motifs in place as shown in photo.

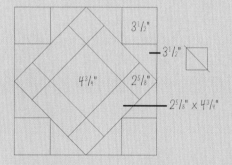

Diagram A

Holly Time Patterns

Holly Leaf

Beak

Bird

Carolers (7½" x 6")

Techniques: Appliquéd, Embroidered

1. Prepare and assemble patterns on page 119. Whipstitch motifs in place as shown in photo above.

2. Embroider eyes as shown in photo. Embroider design as shown in placement below.

fa   la   la

Embroidery Placement

Poinsettia Wreath (10½" x 10½")

Technique: Pieced

1. Using dimensions shown in Diagram A, cut pieces from desired fabrics.

2. Stitch pieces together as shown in photo above.

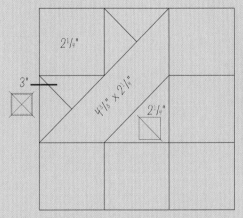

Diagram A

Antique Christmas Star (9½" x 9½")

Technique: Appliquéd

1. Prepare and assemble patterns on page 119.

2. Whipstitch motifs in place as shown in photo at left.

3. Stitch buttons in place as shown.

Christmas Rose (12¼" x 12¼")

Techniques: Pieced, Appliquéd

1. Using dimensions shown in Diagram B, cut pieces from desired fabrics.

2. Stitch pieces together as shown in photo below.

3. Using ½" bias tape for stem, whipstitch motif in place as shown.

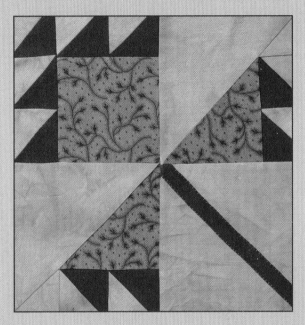

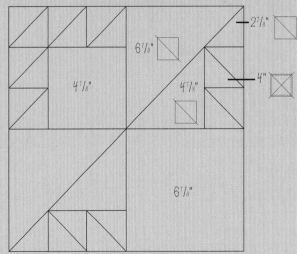

Diagram B

Eight-point Star (5¾" x 7")

Technique: Template Pieced

1. Prepare and assemble template on page 119. Stitch pieces into strips, following numerical sequence.

2. Assemble block by stitching strips together.

Frosty (6" x 9")

Techniques: Appliquéd, Embroidered

1. Prepare and assemble patterns on page 158. Whipstitch motifs in place as shown in photo above.

2. Embroider eyes, nose, mouth, and buttons as shown.

Angel with Garland (8" x 8")

Techniques: Template Pieced, Appliquéd

1. Prepare and assemble template on page 120. Stitch pieces into strips, following numerical sequence.

2. Assemble block by stitching strips together.

3. Prepare and assemble patterns on page 120. Whipstitch motifs in place as shown in photo above.

Cranberry Wreath (10" x 10")

Techniques: Pieced, Appliquéd

1. Using dimensions shown in Diagram A, cut pieces from desired fabrics. Stitch pieces together as shown in photo at left.

2. Prepare and assemble patterns at right. Whipstitch motifs in place as shown in photo.

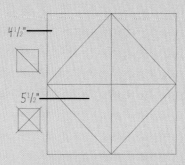

4½"

5½"

Diagram A

Cranberry Wreath Patterns

Berry (9)   Leaf (9)

This pot holder was created using the Cranberry Wreath quilt block above. Three tablespoons of spice potpourri has been placed into the pot holder to scent the air when a hot item is set upon it.

Chapter 3 . . .

Santa Claus Quilt (17" x 22")

Techniques: Template Pieced, Appliquéd, Embroidered

Materials & Tools

Backing fabric (1 yd)

Bias tape: 1"-wide

Coordinating thread

Cotton fabrics: red plaid (½ yd); scraps, assorted colors

Embroidery flosses: black; green; red

Embroidery needle

Fabric scissors

Felt: blue; brown; cream; pink; red

Flannel scraps: green

Iron/ironing board

Muslin (1 yd)

Quilt batting (1 yd)

Sewing machine

Sewing needle

Tape measure

Instructions

1. Prepare and assemble Santa Claus Template, Tree Top Template, and Tree Bottom Template on pages 124–126. Stitch strips together, following numerical sequence on templates.

2. Cut 5" x 6½" rectangle from muslin for upper left-hand corner block.

3. Embroider design as shown in placement on page 123.

4. Stitch blocks together as shown in photo on opposite page.

5. Prepare and assemble patterns on pages 122. Using 3" strip of bias tape for arm, whipstitch motif in place.

6. Cut strips as desired from felt for garland and presents. Whipstitch motifs in place as shown in photo.

7. Embroider candy canes with red stripes and ornaments with hooks as shown.

8. Cut four 1½" x 14½" strips from muslin.

9. Stitch one strip to each side of quilt front. Stitch remaining strips to top and bottom of quilt front.

10. Cut two 2½" x 16½" strips and two 3" x 18" strips from red plaid fabric.

11. Stitch one 2½" strip to each side of quilt front. Stitch 3" strip to top and bottom of quilt front.

12. Cut batting slightly larger than quilt front.

13. Cut backing fabric to size of quilt front.

14. Place quilt front on batting and place both on wrong side of backing. Baste layers together. Quilt layers.

15. Cut two 1¼" x 17¼" and two 1¼" x 22¼" strips from muslin.

16. Stitch one short strip to top and bottom of quilt front for binding. Stitch one long strip to each side of quilt front. Fold and press seam allowance of binding. Fold binding over edges of quilt.

17. Blind-stitch binding to back of quilt.

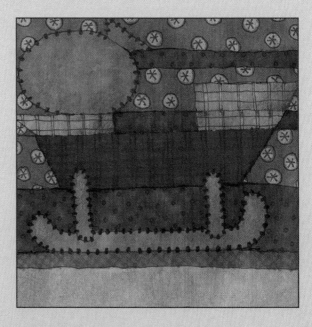

CREATE IT
Sleigh

Techniques: Pieced, Appliquéd

Snowcapped Tree (4³/₄" x 6¹/₂")

Technique: Template Pieced

1. Prepare and assemble template on page 119. Stitch pieces into strips, following numerical sequence.

2. Assemble block by stitching strips together.

Christmas Pinwheels (9¹/₂" x 9¹/₂")

Technique: Pieced

1. Using dimensions shown in Diagram A, cut pieces from desired fabrics.

2. Stitch pieces together as shown in photo above.

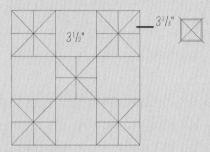

3¹/₂"   3³/₈"

Diagram A

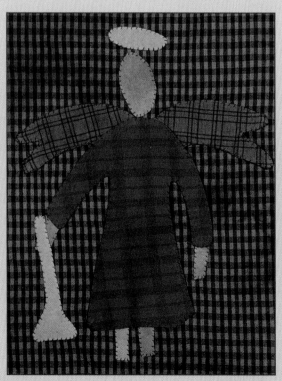

Arch Angel (8³/₄" x 10³/₄")

Technique: Appliquéd

1. Prepare and assemble patterns on page 131.

2. Whipstitch motifs in place as shown in photo at left.

Star in Snow (6½" x 6½")

Technique: Pieced

1. Using dimensions shown in Diagram A, cut pieces from desired fabrics.

2. Stitch pieces together as shown in photo at left.

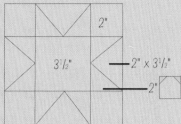

Diagram A

2"

3½"

2" x 3½"

2"

Simple Star on Point (6¾" x 6¾")

Technique: Pieced

1. Using dimensions shown in Diagram B, cut pieces from desired fabrics.

2. Stitch pieces together as shown in photo at right.

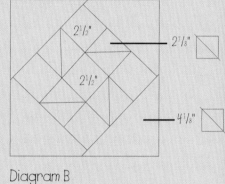

2½"

2⅛"

2½"

4⅛"

Diagram B

Snowball Snowman (6½" x 6½")

Techniques: Pieced, Appliquéd

1. Using dimensions shown in Diagram C, cut pieces from desired fabrics. Stitch pieces together as shown in photo at right.

2. Prepare and assemble patterns at right. Whipstitch motifs in place as shown in photo.

Snowball Snowman Patterns

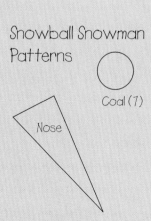

Coal (7)

Nose

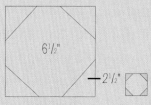

6½"

2½"

Diagram C

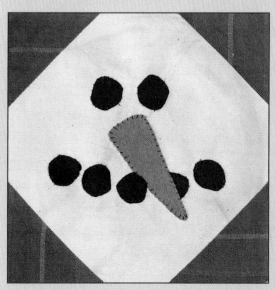

Reindeer Joy (6" x 7½")

Technique: Appliquéd

1. Prepare and assemble patterns on page 130.

2. Whipstitch motifs in place as shown in photo at left.

3. Stitch buttons in place as shown.

CREATE IT

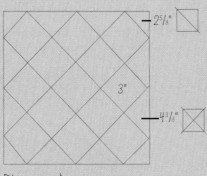

Diagram A

2⅝"

3"

4⅜"

Chimney Sweep (10¾" x 10¾")

Technique: Pieced

1. Using dimensions shown in Diagram A, cut pieces from desired fabrics.

2. Stitch pieces together as shown in photo above.

Down the Chimney (7" x 10")

Techniques: Template Pieced, Appliquéd, Embroidered

1. Prepare and assemble template on page 127. Stitch pieces into strips, following numerical sequence.

2. Assemble block by stitching strips together.

3. Prepare and assemble patterns on page 127. Whipstitch motifs in place as shown in photo at right.

4. Embroider eyes as shown.

Folk-art Reindeer (10" x 10")

Techniques: Pieced, Appliquéd

1. Using dimensions shown in Diagram A, cut pieces from desired fabrics.

2. Stitch pieces together as shown in photo at left.

3. Prepare and assemble patterns on page 130. Whipstitch motifs in place as shown in photo.

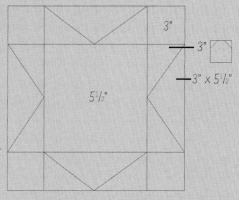

Diagram A

35

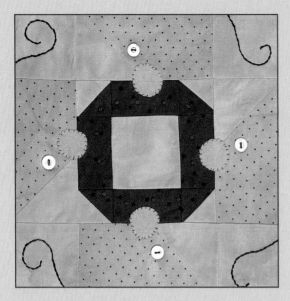

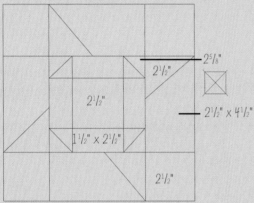

Diagram A

Christmas Mice (8¼" x 8¼")

Techniques: Pieced, Appliquéd, Embroidered

1. Using dimensions shown in Diagram A cut pieces from desired fabrics. Stitch pieces together as shown in photo above.

2. Prepare and assemble patterns below. Whipstitch motifs in place as shown in photo.

3. Embroider tails as shown.

4. Stitch buttons in place as shown.

Christmas Mice Pattern

Ear (4)

Country Christmas Table Runner (39" x 13¼")

Techniques: Pieced, Template Pieced, Appliquéd, Embroidered

Materials & Tools
Backing fabric (1 yd)
Coordinating thread
Cotton fabric: print 3"-square scraps
Embroidery floss: black
Embroidery needle
Fabric scissors
Iron/ironing board
Quilt batting
Quilt blocks: Christmas Mice at left, Simple Holiday Basket page 40, Starlight Trees page 45, Spinning Trees page 107,
Sewing machine
Sewing needle
Tape measure

Instructions
1. Cut five 2½" x 8" strips and two 2½" x 40" strips from backing fabric.

2. Stitch blocks together with one short strip between each block. Stitch remaining short strips to each end. Stitch one long strip to top and bottom of block strip as shown in Diagram B.

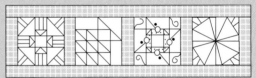

Diagram B

3. Cut batting slightly larger than runner front.

4. Cut backing fabric to size of runner front.

5. Place right side of runner front on batting and place both on right side of backing.

6. Stitch around edge. Trim batting to size.

7. Turn right side out and stitch opening closed.

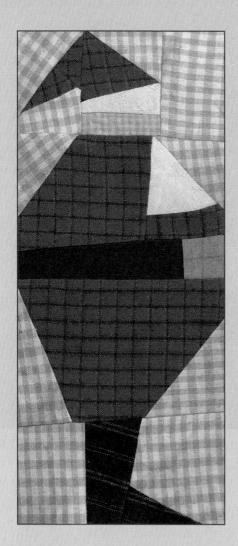

St. Nick (4¼" x 9½")

Technique: Template Pieced

1. Prepare and assemble template on page 157. Stitch pieces into strips, following numerical sequence.

2. Assemble block by stitching strips together.

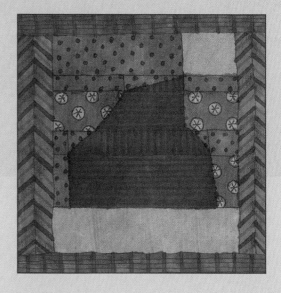

CREATE IT

Santa's Cap

Technique: Template Pieced

Plum Pudding (4¾" x 4¾")

Techniques: Template Pieced, Appliquéd

1. Prepare and assemble template on page 127. Stitch pieces into strips, following numerical sequence.

2. Assemble block by stitching strips together.

3. Prepare and assemble patterns on page 127. Whip-stitch motifs in place as shown in photo at left.

Christmas Top (5¼" x 5¼")

Technique: Template Pieced

1. Prepare and assemble template on page 127. Stitch pieces into strips, following numerical sequence.

2. Assemble block by stitching strips together.

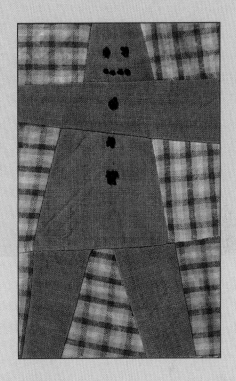

CREATE IT

Ginger Baskets (8¾" x 8¾")

Techniques: Pieced, Appliquéd

1. Using dimensions shown in Diagram A, cut pieces from desired fabrics. Stitch pieces together as shown in photo at right.

2. Prepare and assemble patterns on page 127. Whipstitch motifs in place as shown in photo.

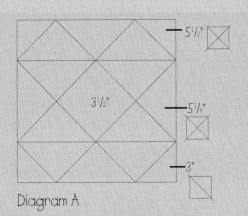

5½"

3½"

5¼"

3"

Diagram A

Crazy-quilt Angel (5½" x 7½")

Techniques: Template Pieced, Appliquéd, Embroidered

1. Prepare and assemble template on page 128. Stitch pieces into strips, following numerical sequence.
2. Assemble block by stitching strips together.
3. Prepare pattern on page 128. Whip-stitch motif in place as shown in photo at left.
4. Embroider on seam lines as shown.

Log Cabin Poinsettia

(5¼" x 5¼")

Technique: Pieced

1. Using dimensions shown in Diagram A, cut pieces from desired fabrics.
2. Stitch pieces together as shown in photo at right.

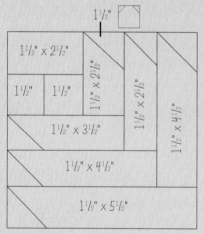

1½"

1½" x 2½"			
1½"	1½"	1½" x 2½"	1½" x 2½"
1½" x 3½"			1½" x 4½"
1½" x 4½"			
1½" x 5½"			

Diagram A

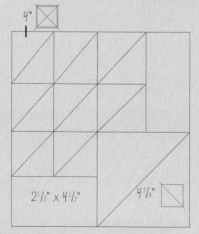

4"

2½" x 4½"   4⅞"

Diagram B

Simple Holiday Basket

(8" x 8")

Technique: Pieced

1. Using dimensions shown in Diagram B, cut pieces from desired fabrics.
2. Stitch pieces together as shown in photo at left.

Farmer Santa (10" x 10")

Techniques: Template Pieced, Appliquéd, Embroidered

1. Prepare and assemble template on page 129. Stitch pieces into strips, following numerical sequence.
2. Assemble block by stitching strips together.
3. Stitch 1/2"-wide log cabin strips around block as shown in photo at left.
4. Prepare and assemble patterns on page 129. Whipstitch motifs in place as shown in photo.
5. Embroider eyes, buttons, and legs on bird as shown.

Snow Angel (7" x 10")

Technique: Appliquéd

1. Prepare and assemble patterns on page 128.
2. Whipstitch motifs in place as shown in photo above.

Snowman with Broom (7¼" x 8¾")

Techniques: Appliquéd, Embroidered

1. Prepare and assemble patterns on page 128. Whipstitch motifs in place as shown in photo above.
2. Embroider eyes, nose, mouth, buttons, and broom as shown.

41

Christmas Heart (3½" x 8")

Techniques: Template Pieced, Appliquéd

1. Prepare and assemble template on page 128. Stitch pieces into strips, following numerical sequence.

2. Assemble block by stitching strips together.

3. Prepare and assemble patterns on page 128. Whipstitch motifs in place as shown in photo at left.

CREATE IT

Crazy-strip Wreath (8½" x 8½")

Technique: Template Pieced

1. Prepare and assemble template on page 157. Stitch pieces into strips, following numerical sequence.

2. Assemble block by stitching strips together.

3. Repeat Steps 1-2 three times.

4. Stitch four blocks together as shown in photo at left.

Christmas Treats (8¼" x 10¼")

Techniques: Template Pieced, Appliquéd, Embroidered

1. Prepare and assemble template on page 130. Stitch pieces into strips, following numerical sequence.

2. Assemble block by stitching strips together.

3. Prepare and assemble patterns on page 130. Whipstitch motifs in place as shown in photo at left.

4. Embroider stripes on candy canes as shown.

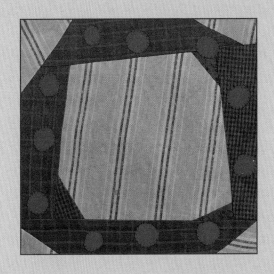

CREATE IT

Twirling Angels (8¼" x 8¼")

Technique: Pieced

1. Using dimensions shown in Diagram A, cut pieces from desired fabrics.

2. Stitch pieces together as shown in photo above.

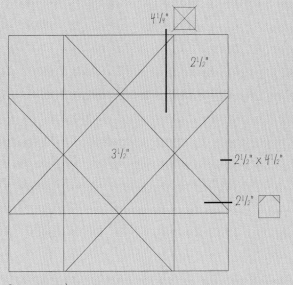

Diagram A

Homespun Snowflake (9¼" x 9¼")

Technique: Pieced

1. Using dimensions shown in Diagram A, cut pieces from desired fabrics.

2. Stitch pieces together as shown in photo at left.

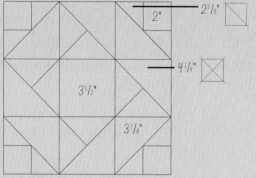

Diagram A

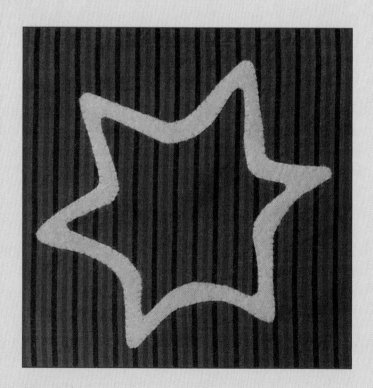

Star Flake (7½" x 7½")

Technique: Appliquéd

1. Prepare pattern on page 130.

2. Whipstitch motif in place as shown in photo above.

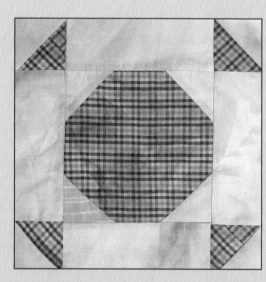

CREATE IT

Starlight Trees (8" x 8")

Techniques: Pieced, Appliquéd

1. Using dimensions shown in Diagram A, cut pieces from desired fabrics.
2. Stitch pieces together as shown in photo at left.
3. Using ½" bias tape for trunks, whipstitch motifs in place as shown.

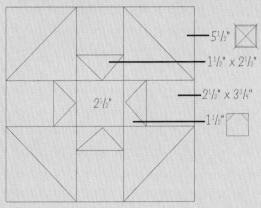

5½" ⊠

1½" x 2½"

2½"

2½" x 3¾"

1½" ☐

Diagram A

Merry Christmas to Moo

(4½" x 7½")

Techniques: Appliquéd, Embroidered

1. Prepare and assemble patterns on page 129. Whipstitch motifs in place as shown in photo above.
2. Embroider eyes, tail, and wreath as shown.

Jolly Santa (7" x 7½")

Techniques: Appliquéd, Embroidered

1. Prepare and assemble patterns on page 129. Whipstitch motifs in place as shown in photo at left.
2. Embroider eyes and mouth as shown.

Chapter 4 . . .

Winter Garden Quilt (26½" x 26½")

Technique: Pieced

Materials & Tools

Backing fabric (¾ yd)
Coordinating thread
Cotton fabrics: 10–12 coordinating (¼ yd each)
Fabric scissors
Iron/ironing board
Quilt batting
Sewing machine
Sewing needle
Tape measure

Instructions

1. Prepare template on page 131 for center.

2. Cut one 1½" x 3½", six 1½" x 4", and one 1½" x 5½" strips from coordinating fabrics for first row.

3. Cut one 1½" x 4", six 1½" x 5", and one 1½" x 6" strips from coordinating fabrics for second row.

4. Cut one 1½" x 4½", six 1½" x 5½", and one 1½" x 7½" strips from coordinating fabrics for third row.

5. Stitch 3½" strip from first row to one side of center. Trim excess on right-hand end as shown in Diagram A.

Diagram A

6. Stitch one 4" strip from first row to next side in clockwise manner. Continue stitching strips around center from first row, cutting each end even with next side as shown in Diagram B.

Diagram B

7. When finished with first row, trim all outside ends for octagon.

8. Repeat Steps 5–7 for second row and third row to complete block.

9. Repeat Steps 1–8 eight times.

10. Cut eighteen 3⅞" squares. Cut in half diagonally.

11. Stitch one triangle in each corner as shown in photo below.

12. Stitch three blocks together in a strip. Repeat two times.

13. Assemble quilt top by stitching strips together as shown in photo on opposite page.

14. Cut batting slightly larger than quilt front.

15. Cut backing fabric to size of quilt front.

16. Place quilt front on batting and place both on wrong side of backing. Baste layers together. Quilt layers.

17. Cut four 1" x 26½" strips from backing fabric.

18. Stitch one strip to each side of quilt front for binding. Fold and press seam allowance of binding. Fold binding over edges of quilt.

19. Blind-stitch binding to back of quilt.

... Winter Wonderland

Forest Friends (13" x 10½")

Techniques: Pieced, Appliquéd

1. Using dimensions shown in Diagram A, cut pieces from desired fabrics.

2. Stitch pieces together as shown in photo at right.

3. Prepare and assemble patterns on page 131. Whipstitch motifs in place as shown in photo.

3½" x 6½"	3½" x 7"
5½"	5½"
2½" x 13"	

2½" x 5½"

Diagram A

CREATE IT

Santa in Sleigh (8" x 9½")

Techniques: Template Pieced, Appliquéd

1. Prepare and assemble template on page 132. Stitch pieces into strips, following numerical sequence.

2. Assemble block by stitching strips together.

3. Prepare and assemble patterns on page 132. Whipstitch motifs in place as shown in photo at left.

48

This pillow was created using the Forest Friends quilt block at the left.

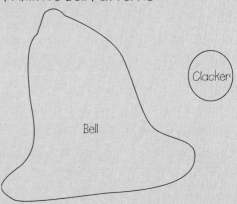

Primitive Bell (5½" x 5½")

Technique: Appliquéd

1. Prepare and assemble patterns below.

2. Whipstitch motifs in place as shown in photo at right.

Primitive Bell Patterns

Clacker

Bell

Pinecone (3¼" x 5½")

Techniques: Template Pieced, Appliquéd, Embroidered

1. Prepare and assemble template on page 133. Stitch pieces into strips, following numerical sequence.

2. Assemble block by stitching strips together.

3. Prepare pattern on page 133. Whipstitch motif in place as shown in photo above.

4. Embroider stem as shown.

Cabin in the Woods (7¼" x 7¼")

Techniques: Template Pieced, Appliquéd

1. Prepare and assemble template on page 134. Stitch pieces into strips, following numerical sequence.

2. Assemble block by stitching strips together.

3. Prepare and assemble patterns on page 134. Whipstitch motifs in place as shown in photo above.

CREATE IT

CREATE IT
Winter Wind
Techniques: Pieced, Embroidered

Mitten (6" x 10")
Technique: Template Pieced
1. Prepare and assemble template on page 133. Stitch pieces into strips, following numerical sequence.
2. Assemble block by stitching strips together.

Pear (4" x 4¼")
Techniques: Template Pieced, Appliquéd, Embroidered
1. Prepare and assemble template on page 133. Stitch pieces into strips, following numerical sequence.
2. Assemble block by stitching strips together.
3. Prepare and assemble patterns on page 133. Whipstitch motifs in place as shown in photo above.
4. Embroider stem as shown.

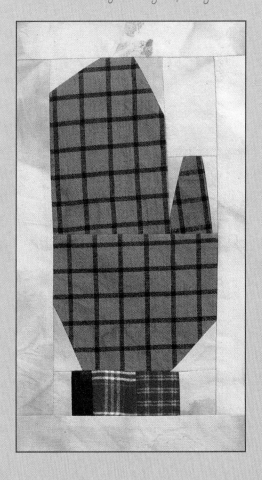

Primitive Snowflake (4³/₄" x 4³/₄")

Techniques: Pieced, Appliquéd

1. Using dimensions shown in Diagram A, cut pieces from desired fabrics.

2. Stitch pieces together as shown in photo at left.

3. Prepare pattern at right. Whipstitch motif in place as shown in photo.

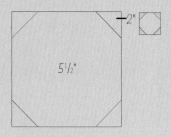

Diagram A

Primitive Snowflake Pattern

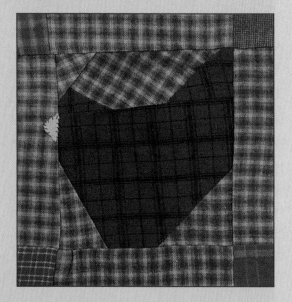

Cardinal (5³/₄" x 6")

Techniques: Template Pieced, Appliquéd

1. Prepare and assemble template on page 134. Stitch pieces into strips, following numerical sequence.

2. Assemble block by stitching strips together.

3. Prepare pattern on page 134. Whipstitch motif in place as shown in photo at left.

Christmas Goose Tracks

(7³/₄" x 7³/₄")

Technique: Pieced

1. Using dimensions shown in Diagram B, cut pieces from desired fabrics.

2. Stitch pieces together as shown in photo at left.

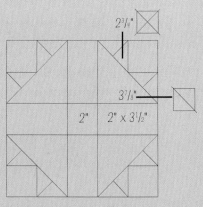

Diagram B

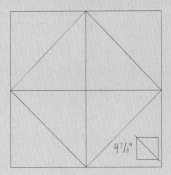

4¹/₈"

Diagram A

Four-patch Trees

(8¹/₂" x 8¹/₂")

Techniques: Pieced, Appliquéd

1. Using dimensions shown in Diagram A, cut pieces from desired fabrics.

2. Stitch pieces together as shown in photo at right.

3. Using ¹/₂" bias tape for trunks, whipstitch motifs in place as shown.

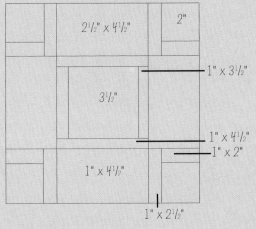

2¹/₂" x 4¹/₂"

2"

1" x 3¹/₂"

3¹/₂"

1" x 4¹/₂"

1" x 2"

1" x 4¹/₂"

1" x 2¹/₂"

Diagram B

Snowflakes

(8¹/₂" x 8¹/₂")

Technique: Pieced

1. Using dimensions shown in Diagram B, cut pieces from desired fabrics.

2. Stitch pieces together as shown in photo at right.

Country Tree (6" x 6")

Technique: Template Pieced

1. Prepare and assemble template on page 134. Stitch pieces into strips, following numerical sequence.

2. Assemble block by stitching strips together.

CREATE IT

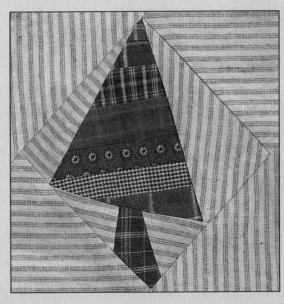

Christmas Farm (7" x 10")

Techniques: Template Pieced, Appliquéd, Embroidered

1. Prepare and assemble template on page 135. Stitch pieces into strips, following numerical sequence.
2. Assemble block by stitching strips together.
3. Prepare and assemble patterns on page 135. Whipstitch motifs in place as shown in photo above.
4. Embroider berries on wreath and beak on chicken as shown.

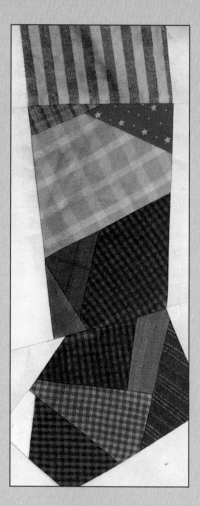

Primitive Stocking (4¼" x 9¾")

Technique: Template Pieced

1. Prepare and assemble template on page 134. Stitch pieces into strips, following numerical sequence.
2. Assemble blocks by stitching strips together.

Santa Claws (5" x 8")

Techniques: Appliquéd, Embroidered

1. Prepare and assemble patterns on page 133. Whipstitch motifs in place as shown in photo above.
2. Embroider nose, whiskers, and center of eyes as shown.

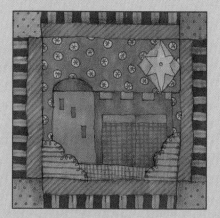

CREATE IT
Bethlehem

Techniques: Pieced, Appliquéd, Embroidered

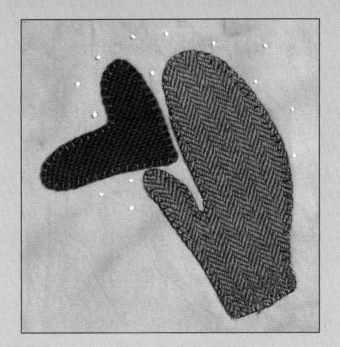

Heart & Mitten (7½" x 7½")

Techniques: Appliquéd, Embroidered

1. Prepare and assemble patterns on page 135. Whipstitch motifs in place as shown in photo above.
2. Embroider base of mitten and snowflakes as shown.

Candy Cane (5" x 10¾")

Technique: Pieced

1. Using dimensions shown in Diagram A, cut pieces from desired fabrics.
2. Stitch pieces together as shown in photo above.

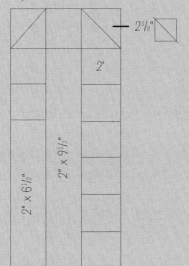

2⅜"

2"

2" x 9½"

2" x 6½"

Diagram A

Bell with Holly (6¼" x 6¼")

Techniques: Template Pieced, Appliquéd, Embroidered

1. Prepare and assemble template on page 135. Stitch pieces into strips, following numerical sequence.
2. Assemble blocks by stitching strips together.
3. Prepare and assemble patterns on page 135. Whipstitch motifs in place as shown in photo above.
4. Embroider clacker stem as shown.

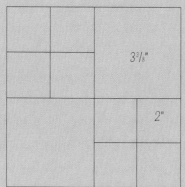

3³/₈"

2"

Diagram A

Four Patch (6¼" x 6¼")

Technique: Pieced

1. Using dimensions shown in Diagram A, cut pieces from desired fabrics.

2. Stitch pieces together as shown in photo at left.

Angel with Star (4¼" x 6½")

Techniques: Template Pieced, Appliquéd

1. Prepare and assemble template on page 138. Stitch pieces into strips, following numerical sequence.

2. Assemble block by stitching strips together.

3. Prepare and assemble patterns on page 138. Whipstitch motifs in place as shown in photo at right.

Choo Choo Train (8" x 7¾")

Techniques: Template Pieced, Appliquéd

1. Prepare and assemble template on page 136. Stitch pieces into strips, following numerical sequence.

2. Assemble block by stitching strips together.

3. Prepare and assemble patterns on page 136. Whipstitch motifs in place as shown in photo at left.

Nutcracker

(3" x 8¾")

Techniques: Template
Pieced, Embroidered

1. Prepare and assemble template on page 136. Stitch pieces into strips, following numerical sequence.

2. Assemble block by stitching strips together.

3. Embroider eyes, nose, and mouth as shown in photo at left.

Starflower *(9½" x 12¾")*

Technique: Appliquéd

1. Prepare and assemble patterns on page 136.

2. Whipstitch motifs in place as shown in photo above.

Star Puzzle *(8½" x 8½")*

Technique: Pieced

1. Using dimensions shown in Diagram A, cut pieces from desired fabrics.

2. Stitch pieces together as shown in photo at left.

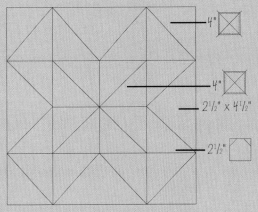

4"

4"

2½" x 4½"

2½"

Diagram A

57

Pieced Snowman (3½" x 7¾")

Techniques: Template Pieced, Embroidered

1. Prepare and assemble template on page 133. Stitch pieces into strips, following numerical sequence.

2. Assemble block by stitching strips together.

3. Embroider eyes, nose, mouth, and buttons as shown in photo below.

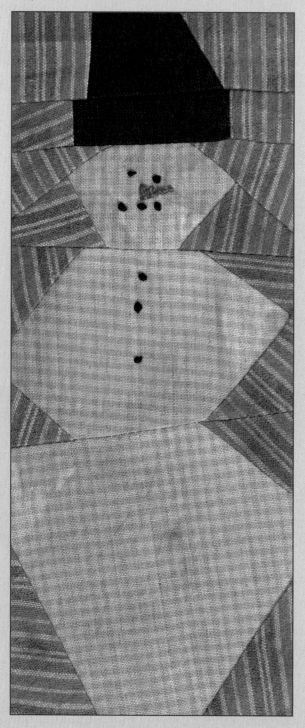

Four-patch Star (8¼" x 8¼")

Techniques: Pieced, Appliquéd

1. Using dimensions shown in Diagram A, cut pieces from desired fabrics.

2. Stitch pieces together as shown in photo above.

3. Prepare pattern below. Whipstitch motifs in place as shown in photo.

Diagram A

Four-patch Star Pattern

This serving tray was created using Four-patch Star quilt block on the opposite page, Twirling Angels quilt block on page 43, Mountain Peaks quilt block on page 64, and Christmas Lights quilt block on page 95. Embellishments such as buttons, lace, old trinkets, and ribbon were added to create a one-of-a-kind look.

Snowman with Stick Tree (6" x 8½")

Techniques: Appliquéd, Embroidered

1. Prepare and assemble patterns on page 136. Whipstitch motifs in place as shown in photo above.

2. Embroider designs as shown in placements on page 136.

Christmas Crow (7" x 12")

Techniques: Appliquéd, Embroidered

1. Prepare and assemble crow patterns on page 137. Whipstitch motifs in place as shown in photo above.

2. Prepare and transfer embroidery patterns on page 137 onto background fabric.

3. Embroider design as shown.

4. Embroider eye as shown in photo.

Blue Santa (4½" x 7½")

Technique: Template Pieced

1. Prepare and assemble template on page 136. Stitch pieces into strips, following numerical sequence.

2. Assemble block by stitching strips together.

Angel with Tree (8" x 8")

Techniques: Template Pieced, Appliquéd, Embroidered

1. Prepare and assemble template on page 137. Stitch pieces into strips, following numerical sequence.

2. Assemble block by stitching strips together.

3. Prepare and assemble patterns on page 137. Whipstitch motifs in place as shown in photo at left.

4. Embroider legs on bird as shown.

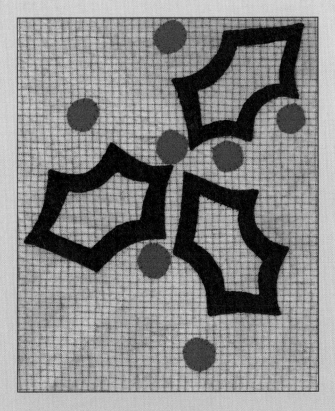

Holly Berry (6½" x 8")

Technique: Appliquéd

1. Prepare and assemble patterns on page 135.

2. Whipstitch motifs in place as shown in photo above.

Christmas Is Heavenly (8½" x 10½")

Technique: Embroidered

1. Prepare and transfer patterns on page 137 onto background fabric.

2. Embroider designs as shown.

Tree in Cabin (9" x 9")

Technique: Template Pieced

1. Prepare and assemble template on page 140. Stitch pieces into strips, following numerical sequence.

2. Assemble block by stitching strips together.

3. Stitch ½"-wide log cabin strips around block as shown in photo at left.

Christmas Tulips (7¼" x 7¼")

Technique: Pieced

1. Using dimensions shown in Diagram A, cut pieces from desired fabrics.

2. Stitch pieces together as shown in photo at right.

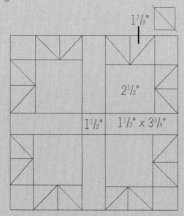

1⅞"

2½"

1½"

1½" x 3¾"

Diagram A

Gold Santa (5³/₄" x 9¹/₂")

Techniques: Template Pieced, Embroidered

1. Prepare and assemble template on page 138. Stitch pieces into strips, following numerical sequence.

2. Assemble block by stitching strips together.

3. Embroider tree as shown in placement at right.

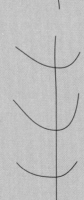

Embroidery Placement

Candlelit Tree (6¹/₂" x 8³/₄")

Techniques: Template Pieced, Embroidered

1. Prepare and assemble template on page 138. Stitch pieces into strips, following numerical sequence. Repeat for reverse side.

2. Assemble block by stitching strips together.

3. Stitch 1¹/₂"-wide log cabin strips around block as shown in photo above.

4. Embroider candles as shown.

CREATE IT

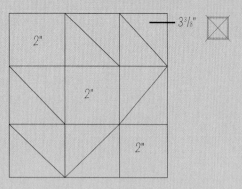

Diagram A

Dove (5" x 5")

Technique: Pieced

1. Using dimensions shown in Diagram A, cut pieces from desired fabrics.

2. Stitch pieces together as shown in photo at right.

CREATE IT
Two Doves

Techniques: Template Pieced, Embroidered

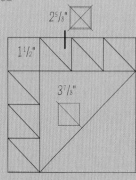

Diagram B

Mountain Peaks (8½" x 8½")

Technique: Pieced

1. Using dimensions shown in Diagram B, cut pieces from desired fabrics.

2. Stitch pieces together as shown in photo above.

3. Repeat Steps 1-2 three times.

4. Stitch four blocks together as shown in photo.

Gingerbread House (7" x 7½")

Techniques: Template Pieced, Appliquéd

1. Prepare and assemble template on page 140. Stitch pieces into strips, following numerical sequence.

2. Assemble block by stitching strips together.

3. Prepare and assemble patterns on page 140. Whipstitch motifs in place as shown in photo at left.

CREATE IT

North Wind (6¼" x 6¼")

Technique: Pieced

1. Using dimensions shown in Diagram A, cut pieces from desired fabrics.

2. Stitch pieces together as shown in photo at right.

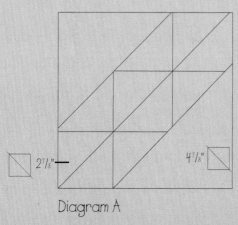

2⅞" 4⅞"

Diagram A

Peace Sheep (5" x 5½")

Techniques: Appliquéd, Embroidered

1. Prepare and assemble patterns on page 132. Whipstitch motifs in place as shown in photo at left.

2. Embroider ears, eyes, and legs as shown in photo. Embroider designs as shown in placements below.

Embroidery Placements

CREATE IT
Pinecones

Technique: Pieced

Merry Hearts (6" x 6")

Technique: Pieced

1. Using dimensions shown in Diagram A, cut pieces from desired fabrics.

2. Stitch pieces together as shown in photo at right.

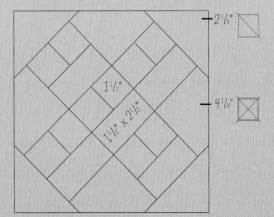

Diagram A

This sachet was created using the Peace Sheep quilt block on the opposite page.

This coaster was created using the Reindeer with Holly quilt block on page 69.

Moose (5¼" x 10½")

Techniques: Template Pieced, Appliquéd

1. Prepare and assemble template on page 139. Stitch pieces into strips, following numerical sequence.

2. Assemble block by stitching strips together.

3. Stitch 1½"-wide log cabin strips around block as shown in photo below.

4. Prepare pattern on page 139. Whipstitch motif in place as shown in photo.

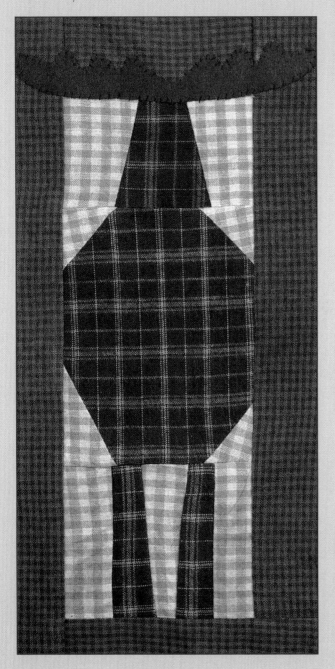

Nine-patch Variation (6½" x 6½")

Technique: Pieced

1. Using dimensions shown in Diagram A, cut pieces from desired fabrics.

2. Stitch pieces together as shown in photo above.

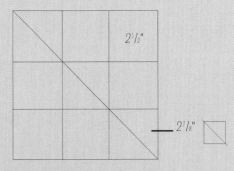

2½"

2⅛"

Diagram A

CREATE IT

Reindeer with Holly (6" x 6½")

Techniques: Appliquéd, Embroidered

1. Prepare pattern on page 138. Whipstitch motif in place as shown in photo at right.
2. Embroider legs as shown in photo. Embroider antlers as shown in placement below.

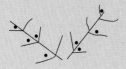

Embroidery Placement

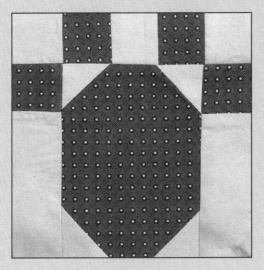

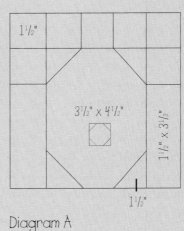

Diagram A

Paw Prints (5¼" x 5¼")

Technique: Pieced

1. Using dimensions shown in Diagram A, cut pieces from desired fabrics.
2. Stitch pieces together as shown in photo at left.

Snowball with Heart (5½" x 5½")

Techniques: Pieced, Appliquéd

1. Using dimensions shown in Diagram B, cut pieces from desired fabrics.
2. Stitch pieces together as shown in photo at left.
3. Prepare and assemble patterns on page 140. Whipstitch motifs in place as shown in photo.

Diagram B

Flying Christmas Trees (5¼" x 5¼")

Technique: Pieced

1. Using dimensions shown in Diagram A, cut pieces from desired fabrics.

2. Stitch pieces together as shown in photo above.

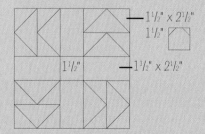

Diagram A

Simple Angel (6¼" x 10¼")

Techniques: Template Pieced, Appliquéd

1. Prepare and assemble template on page 139. Stitch pieces into strips, following numerical sequence.

2. Assemble block by stitching strips together.

3. Prepare and assemble patterns on page 139. Whipstitch motifs in place as shown in photo above.

Half Log Cabin (4½" x 4½")

Technique: Pieced

1. Using dimensions shown in Diagram B, cut pieces from desired fabrics.

2. Stitch pieces together as shown in photo at right.

1½" x 4½"			
1½" x 3½"			
1½" x 2½"		1½" x 2½"	1½" x 3½"
1½"	1½"		

Diagram B

Gingerbread Man with Buttons (6¼" x 6¼")

Techniques: Pieced, Embroidered

1. Using dimensions shown in Diagram A, cut pieces from desired fabrics.

2. Stitch pieces together as shown in photo at left.

3. Embroider cheeks as shown.

4. Stitch buttons in place as shown.

Diagram A

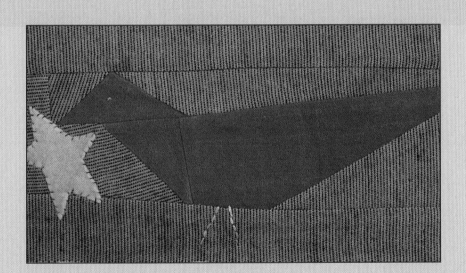

Red Bird with Star (8" x 4¼")

Techniques: Template Pieced, Appliquéd, Embroidered

1. Prepare and assemble template on page 139. Stitch pieces into strips, following numerical sequence.

2. Assemble block by stitching strips together.

3. Prepare pattern on page 139. Whipstitch motif in place as shown in photo above.

4. Embroider eye and legs as shown.

CREATE IT

Chapter 5 . . . .

Snow Bows Quilt (35" x 35")

Technique: Pieced

Materials & Tools

Backing fabric (1¼ yd)

Bleached muslin (1¼ yd)

Cotton fabric: blue print (1¼ yd)

Coordinating thread

Fabric scissors

Iron/ironing board

Quilt batting

Sewing machine

Sewing needle

Tape measure

Instructions

1. Cut thirty-six 3½" squares from muslin.

2. Cut thirty-two 3½" squares from print fabric.

3. Cut thirty-two 2" squares from muslin.

4. Cut sixteen 3⅞" squares from muslin. Cut in half diagonally twice.

5. Cut sixteen 3⅞" squares from print fabric. Cut in half diagonally twice.

6. Snowball corners of 3½" print-fabric squares with 2" muslin squares.

7. Assemble bow block with two 3½" muslin squares and two snowball-cornered squares as shown in Diagram A. Repeat fifteen times.

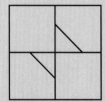

Diagram A

8. Stitch long sides of one print triangle and one muslin triangle together for border block as shown in Diagram B. Repeat thirty-one times.

Diagram B

9. Stitch eight border blocks into a strip as shown in Diagram C. Repeat three times.

Diagram C

10. Stitch one 3½" muslin square to each end of two border-block strips as shown in Diagram D.

Diagram D

11. Stitch four bow blocks into a strip. Repeat three times. Assemble quilt center by stitching bow-block strips together.

12. Stitch one border-block strip without muslin-square ends to each side of quilt center.

13. Stitch border-block strips with muslin ends to top and bottom of quilt center.

14. Cut two 3½" x 34½" and two 3½" x 30" strips from muslin. Stitch one short strip to each side of quilt front. Stitch long strips to top and bottom of quilt.

15. Cut batting to size of quilt front.

16. Cut backing fabric to size of quilt front.

17. Place quilt front on batting and place both on wrong side of backing. Baste layers together. Quilt layers.

18. Cut four 1" x 36" strips from backing fabric.

19. Stitch one strip to each side of quilt front for binding. Fold and press seam allowance of binding. Fold binding over edge of quilt.

20. Blind-stitch binding to back of quilt.

...O' Holy Night

Baby Jesus (6¼" x 7¼")

Techniques: Template Pieced, Appliquéd

1. Prepare and assemble template on page 141. Stitch pieces into strips, following numerical sequence.

2. Assemble block by stitching strips together as shown in photo at left.

3. Prepare and assemble patterns on page 141. Whipstitch motifs in place as shown in photo.

Littlest Angel (4¼" x 4½")

Techniques: Template Pieced, Appliquéd, Embroidered

1. Prepare and assemble template on page 141. Stitch pieces into strips, following numerical sequence.

2. Assemble block by stitching strips together as shown in photo below.

3. Prepare pattern on page 141. Whipstitch motif in place as shown in photo.

4. Embroider eyes and halo as shown.

Gold Star (4¼" x 6½")

Technique: Template Pieced

1. Prepare and assemble template on page 141. Stitch pieces into strips, following numerical sequence.

2. Assemble block by stitching strips together as shown in photo above.

Hearth & Home (8½" x 8½")

Technique: Pieced

1. Using dimensions shown in Diagram A, cut pieces from desired fabrics.

2. Stitch pieces together as shown in photo above.

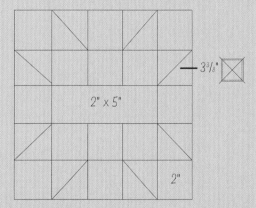

3⅜" ⊠

2" x 5"

2"

Diagram A

Folk-art Snowman (5" x 8½")

Technique: Appliquéd

1. Prepare and assemble patterns on page 145.

2. Whipstitch motifs in place as shown in photo above.

Forever Love (6¼" x 6¼")

Techniques: Template Pieced, Embroidered

1. Prepare and assemble template on page 140. Stitch pieces into strips, following numerical sequence.

2. Assemble block by stitching strips together as shown in photo at right.

3. Prepare and transfer patterns on page 140 onto background fabric.

4. Embroider designs as shown.

5. Embroider on seam lines as shown.

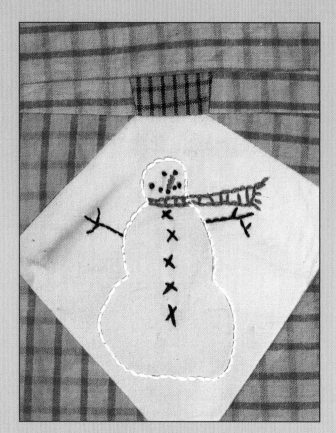

Snowman Ornament (4¾" x 6¼")

Techniques: Template Pieced, Embroidered

1. Prepare and assemble template on page 147. Stitch pieces into strips, following numerical sequence.

2. Assemble block by stitching strips together.

3. Prepare and transfer pattern on page 147. Embroider design as shown in photo at left.

Church (7¼" x 11¼")

Techniques: Template Pieced, Appliquéd, Embroidered

1. Prepare and assemble template on page 146. Stitch pieces into strips, following numerical sequence.

2. Assemble block by stitching strips together.

3. Prepare and assemble patterns on page 146. Whipstitch motifs in place as shown in photo above.

4. Embroider center of door and cross as shown.

Heavenly Star (5" x 7½")

Technique: Template Pieced

1. Prepare and assemble template on page 145. Stitch pieces into strips, following numerical sequence.

2. Assemble block by stitching strips together.

Candle (4¾" x 7")

Techniques: Template Pieced, Appliquéd, Embroidered

1. Prepare and assemble template on page 142. Stitch pieces into strips, following numerical sequence.
2. Assemble block by stitching strips together.
3. Prepare and assemble patterns on page 142. Whipstitch motifs in place as shown in photo at left.
4. Embroider candlewick as shown.

CREATE IT
Star of David

Technique: Template Pieced

Shepherd (5¼" x 8¼")

Techniques: Template Pieced, Appliquéd

1. Prepare and assemble template on page 142. Stitch pieces into strips, following numerical sequence.
2. Assemble block by stitching strips together.
3. Prepare and assemble patterns on page 142. Whipstitch motifs in place as shown in photo at left.

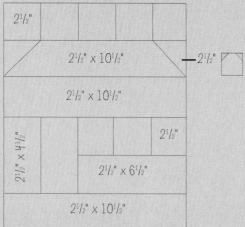

Diagram A

Christmas House

(10¼" x 12¼")

Techniques: Pieced, Appliquéd, Embroidered

1. Using dimensions shown in Diagram A, cut pieces from desired fabrics.

2. Stitch pieces together as shown in photo above.

3. Prepare and assemble patterns on page 141. Whipstitch motifs in place as shown in photo.

4. Embroider wreath and Christmas tree as shown.

5. Stitch button in place as shown.

Dove with Berries (8" x 7½")

Technique: Appliquéd

1. Prepare and assemble patterns on page 142.

2. Whipstitch motifs in place as shown in photo above.

3. Stitch button in place as shown.

Rejoice (8½" x 9")

Techniques: Template Pieced, Appliquéd

1. Prepare and assemble template on page 143. Stitch pieces into strips, following numerical sequence.

2. Assemble block by stitching strips together.

3. Prepare and assemble patterns on page 143. Whipstitch motifs in place as shown in photo above.

Christmas Flower (8¹⁄₄" x 8¹⁄₂")

Techniques: Pieced, Appliquéd

1. Using dimensions shown in Diagram A, cut pieces from desired fabrics.

2. Stitch pieces together as shown in photo at left.

3. Prepare and assemble patterns on page 143. Whipstitch motifs in place as shown in photo.

4¹⁄₂"	

Diagram A

Christmas Town (9" x 6")

Techniques: Template Pieced, Appliquéd

1. Prepare and assemble template on page 144. Stitch pieces into strips, following numerical sequence.

2. Assemble block by stitching strips together.

3. Prepare and assemble patterns on page 144. Whipstitch motifs in place as shown in photo at right.

Noel (8¹⁄₄" x 8¹⁄₂")

Technique: Template Pieced

1. Prepare and assemble template on page 143. Stitch pieces into strips, following numerical sequence.

2. Assemble block by stitching strips together.

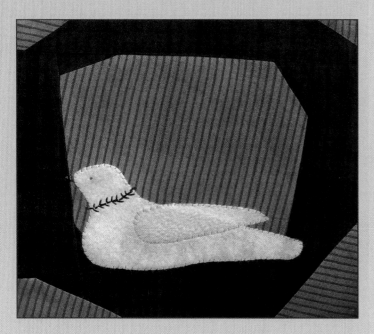

Dove Wreath (8½" x 8")

Techniques: Template Pieced, Appliquéd, Embroidered

1. Prepare and assemble template on page 144. Stitch pieces into strips, following numerical sequence.

2. Assemble block by stitching strips together.

3. Prepare and assemble patterns on page 144. Whipstitch motifs in place as shown in photo above.

4. Embroider beak as shown in photo. Embroider collar as shown in placement below.

Embroidery Placement

Folk-art Angel (5" x 7")

Techniques: Appliquéd, Embroidered

1. Prepare and assemble patterns on page 120. Whipstitch motifs in place as shown in photo above.

2. Embroider eye brows, eyes, mouth, and nose as shown in photo. Embroider designs as shown in placements below.

Embroidery Placements

Holly Basket (9¼" x 9¼")

Techniques: Pieced, Appliquéd

1. Using dimensions shown in Diagram A, cut pieces from desired fabrics.

2. Stitch pieces together as shown in photo at left.

3. Prepare and assemble patterns on page 145. Whipstitch motifs in place as shown in photo.

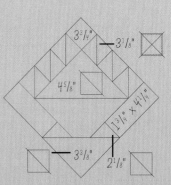

Diagram A

This Christmas ornament was created using the Folk-art Angel quilt block on the opposite page. The completed quilt block was sewn to a solid backing and stuffed with quilt batting. Coordinating ribbon was used for the hanger.

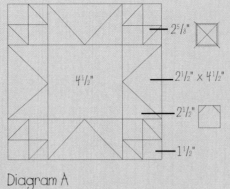

4½"

2⅝"

2½" x 4½"

2½"

1½"

Diagram A

Twinkling Star (8½" x 8½")

Technique: Pieced

1. Using dimensions shown in Diagram A, cut pieces from desired fabrics.

2. Stitch pieces together as shown in photo at left.

Scrap Heart (5½" x 5¼")

Technique: Template Pieced

1. Prepare and assemble template on page 143. Stitch pieces into strips, following numerical sequence.

2. Assemble block by stitching strips together.

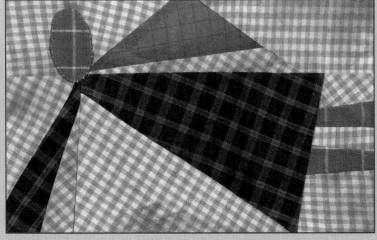

Flying Angel (10¼" x 6½")

Techniques: Template Pieced, Appliquéd

1. Prepare and assemble template on page 158. Stitch pieces into strips, following numerical sequence.

2. Assemble block by stitching strips together.

3. Prepare pattern on page 158. Whipstitch motif in place as shown in photo at left.

Frosty's House (7¼" x 7¼")

Techniques: Template Pieced, Appliquéd, Embroidered

1. Prepare and assemble template on page 132. Stitch pieces into strips, following numerical sequence.
2. Assemble block by stitching strips together.
3. Prepare and assemble patterns on page 132. Whipstitch motifs in place as shown in photo above.
4. Embroider eyes, nose, mouth, and buttons as shown.

CREATE IT

Ships Come Sailing In (4¼" x 4¼")

Technique: Pieced

1. Using dimensions shown in Diagram A, cut pieces from desired fabrics.
2. Stitch pieces together as shown in photo at right.

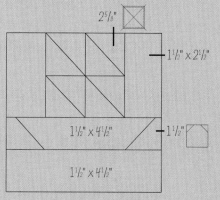

2⅝"

1½" x 2½"

1½" x 4½"

1½"

1½" x 4½"

Diagram A

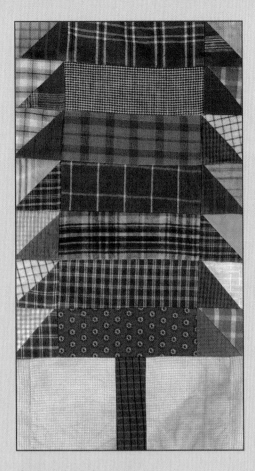

Donkey

Techniques: Template
Pieced, Appliquéd,
Embroidered

Everlasting Pine (7³⁄₄" x 13³⁄₄")

Technique: Pieced

1. Using dimensions shown in Diagram A, cut
   pieces from desired fabrics.

2. Stitch pieces together as shown in
   photo above.

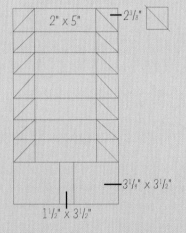

Diagram A

2" x 5"   2³⁄₈"

3¹⁄₄" x 3¹⁄₂"

1¹⁄₂" x 3¹⁄₂"

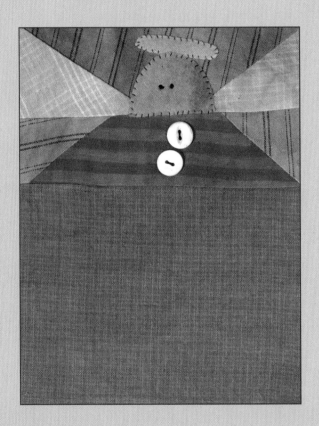

Plump Angel (6" x 8")

Techniques: Template Pieced, Appliquéd, Embroidered

1. Prepare and assemble template on page 145. Stitch pieces
   into strips, following numerical sequence.

2. Assemble block by stitching strips together.

3. Prepare and assemble patterns on page 145. Whipstitch
   motifs in place as shown in photo above.

4. Embroider eyes as shown.

5. Stitch buttons in place as shown.

Christmas Cookies (9" x 9")

Techniques: Pieced, Appliquéd

1. Using dimensions shown in Diagram A, cut pieces from desired fabrics.

2. Stitch pieces together as shown in photo at left.

3. Prepare and assemble patterns on page 146. Buttonhole-stitch motifs in place as shown in photo.

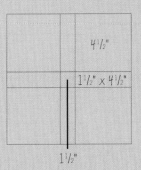

	4½"
1½" x 4½"	

1½"

Diagram A

Pink Angel (4½" x 4½")

Techniques: Template Pieced, Embroidered

1. Prepare and assemble template on page 146. Stitch pieces into strips, following numerical sequence.

2. Assemble block by stitching strips together.

3. Embroider eyes as shown in photo at right.

Star Four Patch (8" x 8")

Technique: Template Pieced

1. Prepare and assemble template on page 145. Stitch pieces into strips, following numerical sequence.

2. Assemble block by stitching strips together.

3. Repeat Steps 1-2 three times.

4. Stitch four blocks together as shown in photo at left.

Chapter 6 . . . .

Crazy Joy Quilt (21" x 21")

Techniques: Template Pieced, Appliquéd, Embroidered

Materials & Tools

Backing fabric

Buttons: black (3)

Coordinating thread

Cotton fabrics: print (2 yds); scraps, 28 coordinating
colors; solid (1 yd)

Embroidery flosses: black; orange; red

Embroidery needle

Felts: brown; green; red; white; yellow

Iron/ironing board

Quilt batting

Sewing machine

Sewing needle

Tape measure

Instructions

1. Prepare and assemble template on
page 148. Stitch strips together, following
numerical sequence. Repeat three times.

2. Stitch four blocks as shown in photo on
opposite page.

3. Prepare and assemble patterns on page 147.
Whipstitch motifs in place as shown in photo.
Embroider stripes on candy canes, berries on
wreath, buttons on snowman, and face on gingerbread man as shown.

4. Cut two 1/8" x 1" strips from brown felt for arms.
Whipstitch motifs onto snowman . Stitch buttons on
gingerbread man as shown.

5. Cut two 1½" x 16½" and two 1½" x 14¾" strips from
solid fabric. Stitch one short strip to each side of
quilt front. Stitch one long strip to top and bottom
of quilt front.

6. Cut two 3½" x 20¼" and two 3½" x 16¼" strips from
print fabric. Stitch one short strip to each side of
quilt front. Stitch one long strip to top and bottom
of quilt front.

7. Cut batting slightly larger than quilt front.

8. Cut backing fabric to size of quilt front.

9. Place quilt front on batting and place both on wrong side of backing.
Baste layers together. Quilt layers of two outer rows around blocks.

10. Using embroidery floss, tie-quilt and knot center of each template-
pieced fabric. Trim floss to ⅜".

11. Cut four 1" x 21" from print fabric.

12. Stitch one strip to each side of quilt front for binding. Fold and
press seam allowance of binding. Fold binding over edges of quilt.

13. Blind-stitch binding to back of quilt.

Crazy-quilt Heart (6½" x 5")

Techniques: Template Pieced, Embroidered

1. Prepare and assemble template on page 119. Stitch pieces into strips,
following numerical sequence.

2. Assemble block by stitching strips together as shown in photo above.

3. Embroider on seam lines as shown.

Antique Santa (5½" x 8")

Techniques: Template Pieced, Appliquéd

1. Prepare and assemble template on page 149. Stitch pieces into strips, following numerical sequence.

2. Assemble block by stitching strips together.

3. Prepare pattern on page 149. Whipstitch motif in place as shown in photo above.

Folk-art Star (8" x 7¼")

Techniques: Appliquéd

1. Prepare and assemble patterns on page 149.

2. Buttonhole-stitch motifs in place as shown in photo below.

Star Basket (6¼" x 6¼")

Techniques: Pieced, Appliquéd

1. Using dimensions shown in Diagram A, cut pieces from desired fabrics.

2. Stitch pieces together as shown in photo at left.

3. Prepare patterns at right. Whipstitch motifs in place as shown in photo.

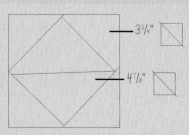

Diagram A

Star Basket Pattern

Wool Tree (3½" x 6")

Technique: Appliquéd

1. Prepare and assemble patterns on page 158.
2. Whipstitch motifs in place as shown in photo at left.

CREATE IT
Star of East

Technique.s: Template Pieced, Appliquéd

Chimney & Cobble Stones (8¼" x 8¼")

Technique: Pieced

1. Using dimensions shown in Diagram A, cut pieces from desired fabrics.
2. Stitch pieces together as shown in photo at right.

1½" x 6½"		
1½" x 4½"		
1½" x 2½"		
2½"		
	1½"	
		1½"

Diagram A

Tin Soldier (6¼" x 6½")

Technique: Pieced

1. Using dimensions shown in Diagram A, cut pieces from desired fabrics.
2. Stitch pieces together as shown in photo at left.

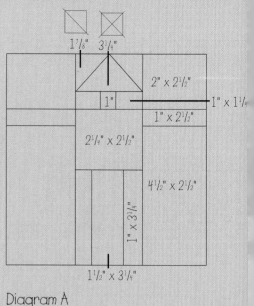

1⅞"   3¼"

2" x 2½"

1"

1" x 1¼

1" x 2½"

2¼" x 2½"

4½" x 2½"

1" x 3¼"

1½" x 3¼"

Diagram A

Meowy Christmas (5½" x 9")

Technique: Embroidered

1. Prepare and transfer patterns on page 149 onto background fabric.
2. Embroider designs as shown.

Toy Drum (6" x 5½")

Technique: Template Pieced

1. Prepare and assemble template on page 150. Stitch pieces into strips, following numerical sequence.
2. Assemble block by stitching strips together.

Basket with Holly (6¼" x 6½")

Techniques: Template Pieced, Appliquéd

1. Prepare and assemble template on page 150. Stitch pieces into strips, following numerical sequence.

2. Assemble block by stitching strips together.

3. Prepare and assemble patterns on page 150. Whipstitch motifs in place as shown in photo at left.

Holiday Bell (6½" x 6½")

Techniques: Template Pieced, Appliquéd, Embroidered

1. Prepare and assemble template on page 150. Stitch pieces into strips, following numerical sequence.

2. Assemble block by stitching strips together.

3. Prepare and assemble patterns on page 150. Whipstitch motifs in place as shown in photo at left.

4. Embroider stem on clacker as shown.

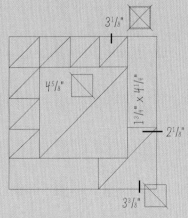

Diagram A

Fruit Basket (6¾" x 6¾")

Techniques: Pieced, Appliquéd

1. Using dimensions shown in Diagram A, cut pieces from desired fabrics.

2. Stitch pieces together as shown in photo at left.

3. Prepare and assemble patterns on page 150. Whipstitch motifs in place as shown in photo.

Wool Snow Flake (10" x 10")

Technique: Appliquéd

1. Prepare and assemble patterns on page 141.

2. Whipstitch motifs in place as shown in photo at left.

CREATE IT

Plain Santa (7½" x 12")

Techniques: Appliquéd, Embroidered

1. Prepare and assemble patterns on page 149. Whipstitch motifs in place as shown in photo at right.

2. Embroider eyes and belt buckle as shown.

3. Stitch buttons in place as shown.

This bulletin board was created using Wool Snow Flake quilt block on the opposite page, Folk-art Reindeer on page 35, Farmer Santa quilt block on page 41, Christmas Treats quilt block on page 43, and Angel with Tree quilt block on page 61. Each velvet-trimmed quilt block has been fused to the bulletin board.

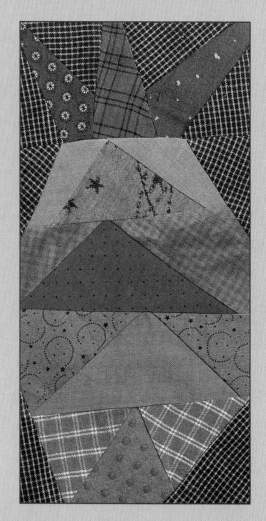

Pieced Pineapple (5¼" x 10")

Technique: Template Pieced

1. Prepare and assemble template on page 151. Stitch pieces into strips, following numerical sequence.

2. Assemble block by stitching strips together.

Star Garland (6½" x 5")

Techniques: Pieced, Embroidered

1. Using dimensions shown in Diagram A, cut pieces from desired fabrics.

2. Prepare and transfer patterns on page 126 onto background fabric.

3. Embroider designs as shown.

4. Stitch pieces together as shown in photo above.

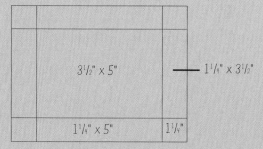

3½" x 5"   1¼" x 3½"

1¼" x 5"   1¼"

Diagram A

Rose Poinsettia

(9¼" x 9¼")

Techniques: Template Pieced, Pieced

1. Prepare template on page 126.

2. Using dimensions shown in Diagram B, cut pieces from desired fabrics.

3. Stitch pieces together in a clockwise manner around template as shown in photo at right.

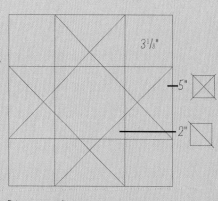

3⅛"

5"

2"

Diagram B

Pear Tree (6" x 8¼")

Techniques: Template Pieced, Appliquéd, Embroidered

1. Prepare and assemble template on page 152. Stitch pieces into strips, following numerical sequence.
2. Assemble block by stitching strips together.
3. Prepare and assemble patterns on page 152. Whipstitch motifs in place as shown in photo at left.
4. Embroider legs on birds and hooks as shown.

Snowman with Boots (6" x 7½")

Techniques: Appliquéd, Embroidered

1. Prepare and assemble patterns on page 154. Whipstitch motifs in place as shown in photo at right.
2. Embroider eyes and mouth as shown.

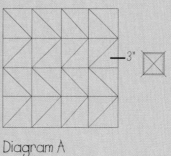

Diagram A

Christmas Lights (8¼" x 8¼")

Technique: Pieced

1. Using dimensions shown in Diagram A, cut pieces from desired fabrics.
2. Stitch pieces together as shown in photo at left.

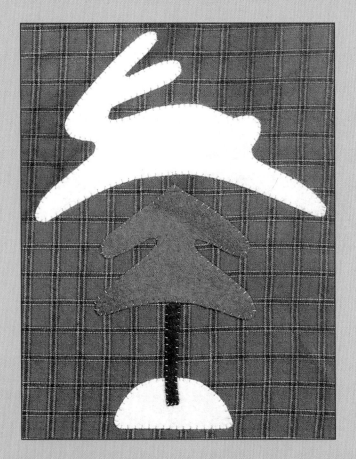

Snowbunny (7" x 9")

Technique: Appliquéd

1. Prepare and assemble patterns on page 152.

2. Whipstitch motifs in place as shown in photo above.

CREATE IT

Rocking Horse (8" x 8½")

Techniques: Template Pieced, Appliquéd

1. Prepare and assemble template on page 153. Stitch pieces into strips, following numerical sequence.

2. Assemble block by stitching strips together.

3. Prepare and assemble patterns on page 153. Whipstitch motifs in place as shown in photo at right.

4. Stitch button in place as shown.

Mistletoe (7¼" x 7¼")

Techniques: Pieced, Appliquéd

1. Using dimensions shown in Diagram A, cut pieces from desired fabrics.

2. Stitch pieces together as shown in photo at left.

3. Prepare and assemble patterns on page 153. Whipstitch motifs in place as shown in photo.

4"	

Diagram A

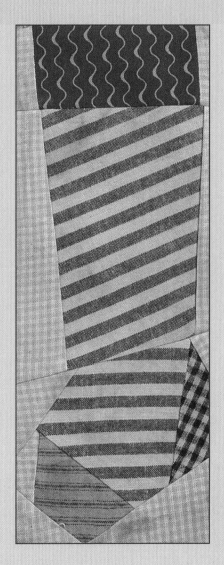

Primitive Candy Cane

(4½" x 8½")

Technique: Template Pieced

1. Prepare and assemble template on page 138. Stitch pieces into strips, following numerical sequence.

2. Assemble block by stitching strips together.

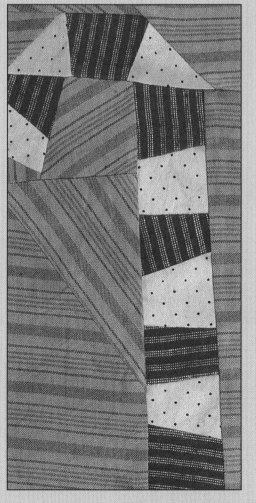

Stocking (4¼" x 10")

Technique: Template Pieced

1. Prepare and assemble template on page 153. Stitch pieces into strips, following numerical sequence.

2. Assemble block by stitching strips together.

St. Nick with Tree (8" x 8")

Techniques: Template Pieced, Appliquéd

1. Prepare and assemble template on page 154. Stitch pieces into strips, following numerical sequence.

2. Assemble block by stitching strips together.

3. Prepare and assemble patterns on page 154. Whipstitch motifs in place as shown in photo above.

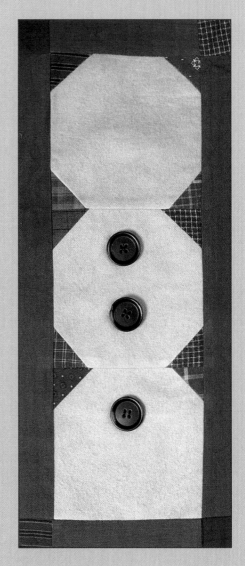

CREATE IT

Holly Heart (8¼" x 7")

Techniques: Template Pieced, Appliquéd

1. Prepare and assemble template on page 154. Stitch pieces into strips, following numerical sequence.

2. Assemble block by stitching strips together.

3. Prepare and assemble patterns on page 154. Whipstitch motifs in place as shown in photo at left.

4. Stitch buttons in place as shown.

Mistletoe Wreath (7½" x 7½")

Techniques: Pieced, Embroidered, Appliquéd,

1. Using dimensions shown in Diagram A, cut pieces from desired fabrics.
2. Prepare and transfer embroidery pattern on page 153 onto background fabric.
3. Embroider design as shown.
4. Prepare and assemble leaf and berry patterns on page 153. Whipstitch motifs in place as shown in photo at left.
5. Stitch pieces together as shown.

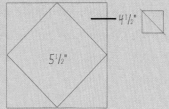

Diagram A

Jingle Bells (8½" x 5½")

Techniques: Appliquéd, Embroidered

1. Prepare and assemble bell patterns on page 152. Whipstitch motifs in place as shown in photo above.
2. Prepare and transfer embroidery patterns on page 152 onto background fabric.
3. Embroider designs as shown.

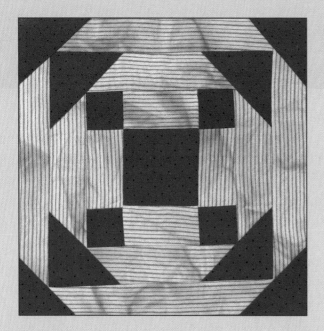

Holiday Cabin (8¼" x 8¼")

Technique: Pieced

1. Using dimensions shown in Diagram A, cut pieces from desired fabrics.

2. Stitch pieces together as shown in photo at left.

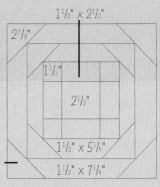

Diagram A

Christmas Hand & Heart (7¼" x 7¼")

Technique: Appliquéd

1. Prepare and assemble patterns on page 151.

2. Whipstitch motifs in place as shown in photo at right.

Reindeer Face (4½" x 4½")

Technique: Template Pieced

1. Prepare and assemble template on page 150. Stitch pieces into strips, following numerical sequence.

2. Assemble block by stitching strips together.

3. Stitch buttons in place as shown in photo at left.

This pillow pocket was created using the Christmas Hand & Heart Quilt block on the opposite page.

Rolling Snowball (7½" x 7½")

Technique: Pieced

1. Using dimensions shown in Diagram A, cut pieces from desired fabrics.
2. Stitch pieces together as shown in photo at left.

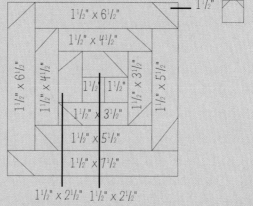

1½" x 6½"   1½"

1½" x 4½"

1½" x 6½"   1½" x 4½"   1½" x 3½"   1½" x 5½"

1½"   1½"

1½" x 3½"

1½" x 5½"

1½" x 7½"

1½" x 2½"   1½" x 2½"

Diagram A

Joy Wreath (8½" x 8½")

Techniques: Pieced, Appliquéd

1. Using dimensions shown in Diagram B, cut pieces from desired fabrics.
2. Stitch pieces together as shown in photo at left.
3. Prepare and assemble patterns on page 151. Whipstitch motifs in place as shown in photo.

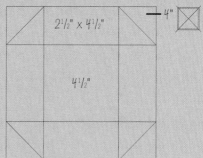

2½" x 4½"   4"

4½"

Diagram B

Little Santa (4¼" x 4½")

Techniques: Template Pieced, Embroidered

1. Prepare and assemble template on page 152. Stitch pieces into strips, following numerical sequence.
2. Assemble block by stitching strips together.
3. Embroider eyes as shown in photo at left.

CREATE IT

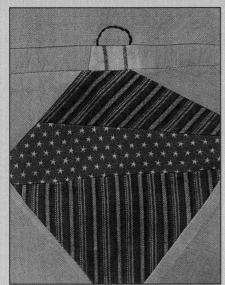

CREATE IT

Star Ornament (4¾" x 5¾")

Techniques: Template Pieced, Appliquéd, Embroidered

1. Prepare and assemble template on page 152. Stitch pieces into strips, following numerical sequence.
2. Assemble block by stitching strips together.
3. Prepare pattern on page 152. Whipstitch motif in place as shown in photo at right.
4. Embroider hook as shown.

Gingerbread Man (5" x 5")

Technique: Appliquéd

1. Prepare pattern on page 153.

2. Whipstitch motif in place as shown in photo above.

3. Stitch buttons in place as shown.

CREATE IT
Snow Cap

Techniques: Appliquéd, Embroidered

Little Snowball (3½" X 3½")

Technique: Pieced

1. Using dimensions shown in Diagram A, cut pieces from desired fabrics.

2. Stitch pieces together as shown in photo above.

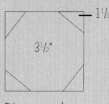

Diagram A

Roly-Poly Snowman (7" x 8½")

Techniques: Appliquéd, Embroidered

1. Prepare and assemble patterns on page 154.

2. Whipstitch motifs in place as shown in photo at left.

3. Embroider eyes, mouth, and buttons as shown.

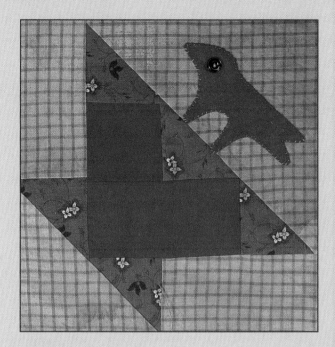

Red Bird Basket $(8\frac{1}{4}" \times 8\frac{1}{4}")$

Techniques: Pieced, Appliquéd

1. Using dimensions shown in Diagram A, cut pieces from desired fabrics.

2. Stitch pieces together as shown in photo above.

3. Prepare pattern below. Whipstitch motif in place as shown in photo.

4. Stitch button in place as shown.

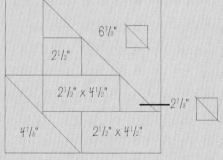

Diagram A

Red Bird Basket Pattern

Crazy Candy Cane $(8\frac{1}{2}" \times 8\frac{1}{2}")$

Technique: Template Pieced

1. Prepare and assemble template on page 150. Stitch pieces into strips, following numerical sequence.

2. Assemble blocks by stitching strips together.

3. Repeat Steps 1–2 three times.

4. Stitch four blocks together as shown in photo below.

CREATE IT

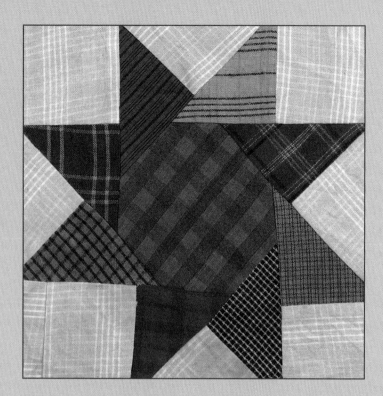

Twisting Star $(8^{3}/_{4}" \times 8^{3}/_{4}")$

Techniques: Template Pieced, Pieced

1. Prepare template on page 157.

2. Using dimensions shown in Diagram A, cut pieces from desired fabrics.

3. Stitch pieces together in a clockwise motion around template as shown in photo at left.

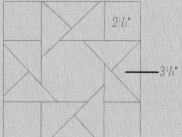

$2^{1}/_{2}"$

$3^{1}/_{8}"$

Diagram A

Winter Cabin $(7^{3}/_{4}" \times 7^{1}/_{2}")$

Techniques: Appliquéd, Embroidered

1. Prepare and assemble patterns on page 155. Whipstitch motifs in place as shown in photo at left.

2. Embroider snowflakes, chimney smoke, and legs on bird as shown.

Cranberry Basket (6" x 6½")

Techniques: Appliquéd, Embroidered

1. Prepare and assemble patterns on page 155. Whipstitch motifs in place as shown in photo at left.

2. Embroider design as shown in placement below.

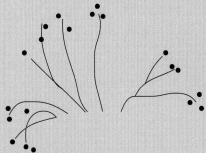

Embroidery Placement

CREATE IT
Stable

Techniques: Appliquéd, Embroidered

Spinning Trees (8" x 8")

Technique: Template Pieced

1. Prepare and assemble template on page 156. Stitch pieces into strips, following numerical sequence.

2. Assemble block by stitching strips together.

3. Repeat Steps 1-2 three times.

4. Stitch four blocks together as shown in photo at right.

Poinsettia Basket (7" x 7¾")

Techniques: Template Pieced, Appliquéd

1. Prepare and assemble template on page 151. Stitch pieces into strips, following numerical sequence.

2. Assemble block by stitching strips together.

3. Prepare and assemble patterns on page 151. Whipstitch motifs in place as shown in photo at left.

Star Stairway (9¼" x 9¼")

Technique: Pieced

1. Using dimensions shown in Diagram A, cut pieces from desired fabrics.

2. Stitch pieces together as shown in photo at right.

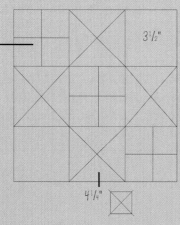

2"

3½"

4¼"

Diagram A

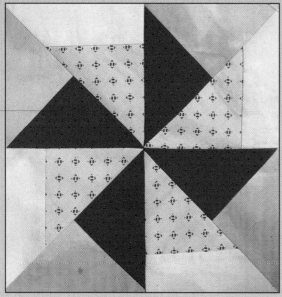

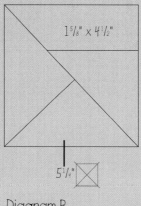

1⅝" x 4½"

5¼"

Diagram B

Peppermint Candy (8¼" x 8¼")

Technique: Pieced

1. Using dimensions shown in Diagram B, cut pieces from desired fabrics.

2. Stitch pieces together as shown in photo at left.

3. Repeat Steps 1–2 three times.

4. Stitch four blocks together as shown in photo.

This rustic frame was created using the Christmas Angel Block on page 110, Wreath Block on page 110, Snowman Block on page 110, and Star Block on page 111. Fabric strips were stitched between blocks, making one large block. This large block was then mounted and framed.

Christmas Angel Block

(6¼" x 6¼")

Techniques: Pieced, Appliquéd Embroidered

1. Using dimensions shown in Diagram A, cut pieces from desired fabrics.

2. Stitch pieces together as shown in photo above.

3. Prepare and assemble patterns on page 155. Whipstitch motifs in place as shown in photo.

4. Embroider eyes as shown.

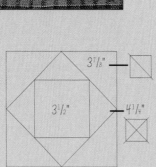

Diagram A

Wreath Block (6¼" x 6¼")

Techniques: Pieced, Appliquéd, Embroidered

1. Using dimensions shown in Diagram A, cut pieces from desired fabrics.

2. Stitch pieces together as shown in photo above.

3. Prepare pattern at right. Whipstitch motif in place as shown in photo.

4. Embroider berries as shown.

Wreath Block Pattern

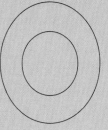

Snowman Block (6¼" x 6¼")

Techniques: Pieced, Appliquéd, Embroidered

1. Using dimensions shown in Diagram A, cut pieces from desired fabrics.

2. Stitch pieces together as shown in photo at left.

3. Prepare and assemble patterns on page 155. Whipstitch motifs in place as shown in photo.

4. Embroider eyes, nose, mouth, and buttons as shown.

110

Star Block (6¼" x 6¼")

Techniques: Pieced, Appliquéd

1. Using dimensions shown in Diagram A on opposite page, cut pieces from desired fabrics.
2. Stitch pieces together as shown in photo at left.
3. Prepare pattern below. Whipstitch motif in place as shown in photo.

Star Block Pattern

CREATE IT

Stocking Block (6¼" x 6¼")

Techniques: Pieced, Appliquéd, Embroidered

1. Using dimensions shown in Diagram A on opposite page, cut pieces from desired fabrics.
2. Stitch pieces together as shown in photo at left.
3. Prepare and assemble patterns on page 155. Whipstitch motifs in place as shown in photo.
4. Embroider stripes on candy cane as shown.

111

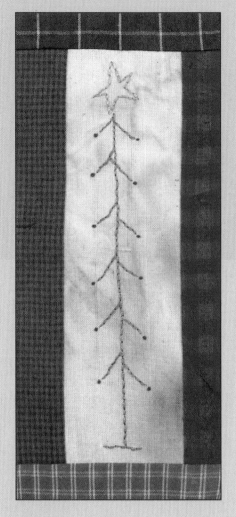

$1^1/_2" \times 4^1/_2"$

$1^1/_2" \times 9"$ $3" \times 9"$

Diagram A

Tumbling Santa $(8^1/_4" \times 8^1/_4")$

Techniques: Template Pieced, Embroidered

1. Prepare and assemble template on page 156. Stitch pieces into strips, following numerical sequence.

2. Assemble block by stitching strips together.

3. Repeat Steps 1–2 three times.

4. Stitch four blocks together as shown in photo above.

5. Embroider eyes as shown.

Feather Tree $(6^1/_2" \times 9")$

Techniques: Pieced, Embroidered

1. Using dimensions shown in Diagram A, cut pieces from desired fabrics.

2. Prepare and transfer pattern on page 155 onto background fabric.

3. Embroider designs as shown.

4. Stitch pieces together as shown in photo above.

Liberty Angel $(8" \times 8^1/_4")$

Techniques: Template Pieced, Appliquéd

1. Prepare and assemble template on page 156. Stitch pieces into strips, following numerical sequence.

2. Assemble block by stitching strips together.

3. Prepare and assemble patterns on page 156. Whipstitch motifs in place as shown in photo at left.

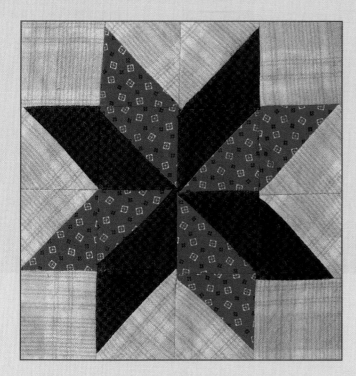

Poinsettia (6½" x 6½")

Technique: Pieced

1. Using dimensions shown in Diagram A, cut pieces from desired fabrics.

2. Stitch pieces together as shown in photo at left.

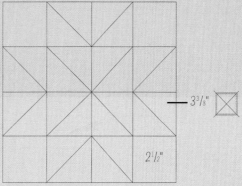

— 3⅜"

2½"

Diagram A

Holly Wreath (8½" x 8½")

Techniques: Pieced, Appliquéd

1. Using dimensions shown in Diagram B, cut pieces from desired fabrics.

2. Stitch pieces together as shown in photo below.

3. Prepare and assemble patterns below. Whipstitch motifs in place as shown in photo.

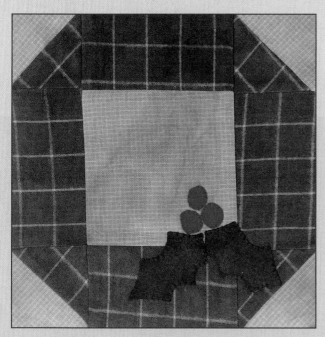

CREATE IT

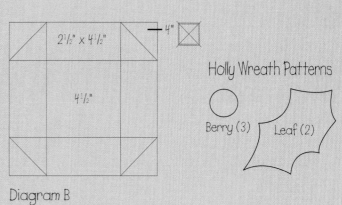

— 4"

2½" x 4½"

4½"

Diagram B

Holly Wreath Patterns

Berry (3)   Leaf (2)

113

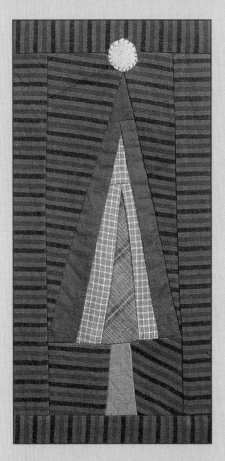

	1½" x 2½"	1½" x 3½"	
1½" x 3½"		1½" x 2½"	1½" x 2½"
	1½" x 3½"		1½" x 2½"	1½"
1½" x 3½"		1½" x 3½"		1½" x 2½"
	1½" x 2½"		1½" x 3½"	
		1½"		2½"

Diagram A

Christmas Pine Tree (5¼" x 10½")

Techniques: Template Pieced, Appliquéd

1. Prepare and assemble template on page 156. Stitch pieces into strips, following numerical sequence.

2. Assemble block by stitching strips together.

3. Prepare pattern on page 156. Whipstitch motif in place as shown in photo above.

Log Cabin Tree (6½" x 6½")

Techniques: Pieced, Appliquéd

1. Using dimensions shown in Diagram A, cut pieces from desired fabrics.

2. Stitch pieces together as shown in photo above.

3. Prepare pattern on page 155. Whipstitch motif in place as shown in photo.

CREATE IT

Church

Technique: Template Pieced

Tree on Point (5¾" x 5¾")

Techniques: Pieced, Appliquéd

1. Using dimensions shown in Diagram A, cut pieces from desired fabrics.

2. Stitch pieces together as shown in photo below.

3. Prepare pattern below. Whipstitch motif in place as shown in photo.

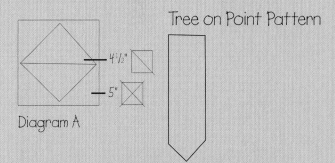

Diagram A

Tree on Point Pattern

Plump Santa (6¼" x 8")

Techniques: Template Pieced, Appliquéd, Embroidered

1. Prepare and assemble template on page 157. Stitch pieces into strips, following numerical sequence.

2. Assemble block by stitching strips together.

3. Prepare and assemble patterns on page 157. Whipstitch motifs in place as shown in photo above.

4. Embroider eyes as shown.

5. Stitch buttons in place as shown.

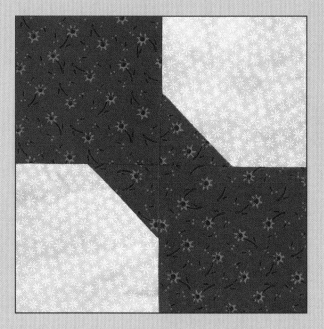

Christmas Bow

(6½" x 6½")

Technique: Pieced

1. Using dimensions shown in Diagram B, cut pieces from desired fabrics.

2. Stitch pieces together as shown in photo at left.

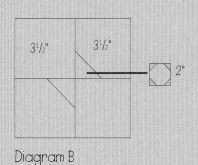

Diagram B

Patterns & Templates

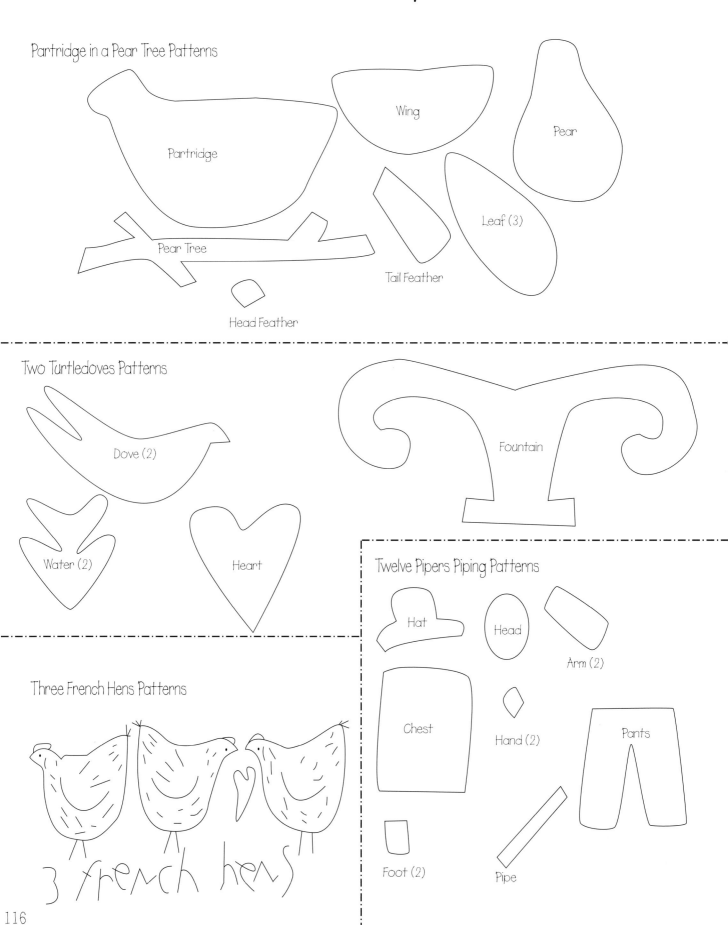

Partridge in a Pear Tree Patterns

Partridge

Wing

Pear

Leaf (3)

Pear Tree

Tail Feather

Head Feather

Two Turtledoves Patterns

Dove (2)

Fountain

Water (2)

Heart

Twelve Pipers Piping Patterns

Hat

Head

Arm (2)

Chest

Hand (2)

Pants

Three French Hens Patterns

3 french hens

Foot (2)

Pipe

116

Eight Maids-a-Milking Template

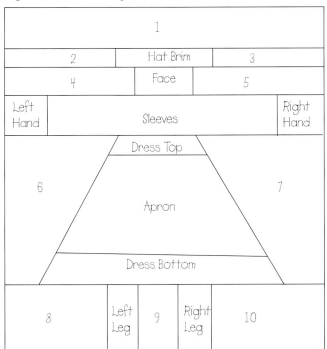

1		
2	Hat Brim	3
4	Face	5

| Left Hand | Sleeves | Right Hand |

| 6 | Dress Top / Apron / Dress Bottom | 7 |

| 8 | Left Leg | 9 | Right Leg | 10 |

Eight Maids-a-Milking Patterns

Hat

Milk Pail

Milk Pail Handle

Nine Ladies Dancing Patterns

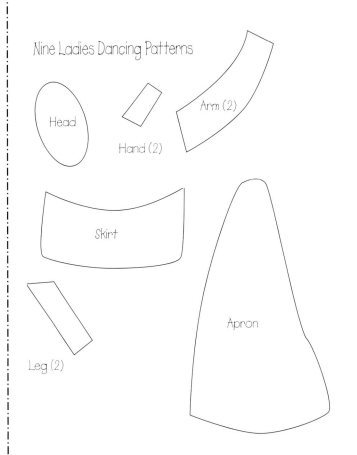

Head

Hand (2)

Arm (2)

Skirt

Leg (2)

Apron

Ten Drummers Drumming Template

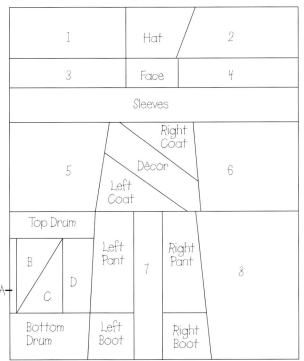

| 1 | Hat | 2 |
| 3 | Face | 4 |

Sleeves

| 5 | Right Coat / Décor / Left Coat | 6 |

Top Drum

| B | | Left Pant | Right Pant | |
| A→ C | D | | 7 | 8 |

| Bottom Drum | Left Boot | Right Boot |

Eleven Lords-a-Leaping Patterns

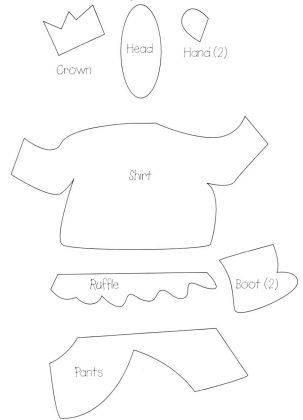

Crown

Head

Hand (2)

Shirt

Ruffle

Boot (2)

Pants

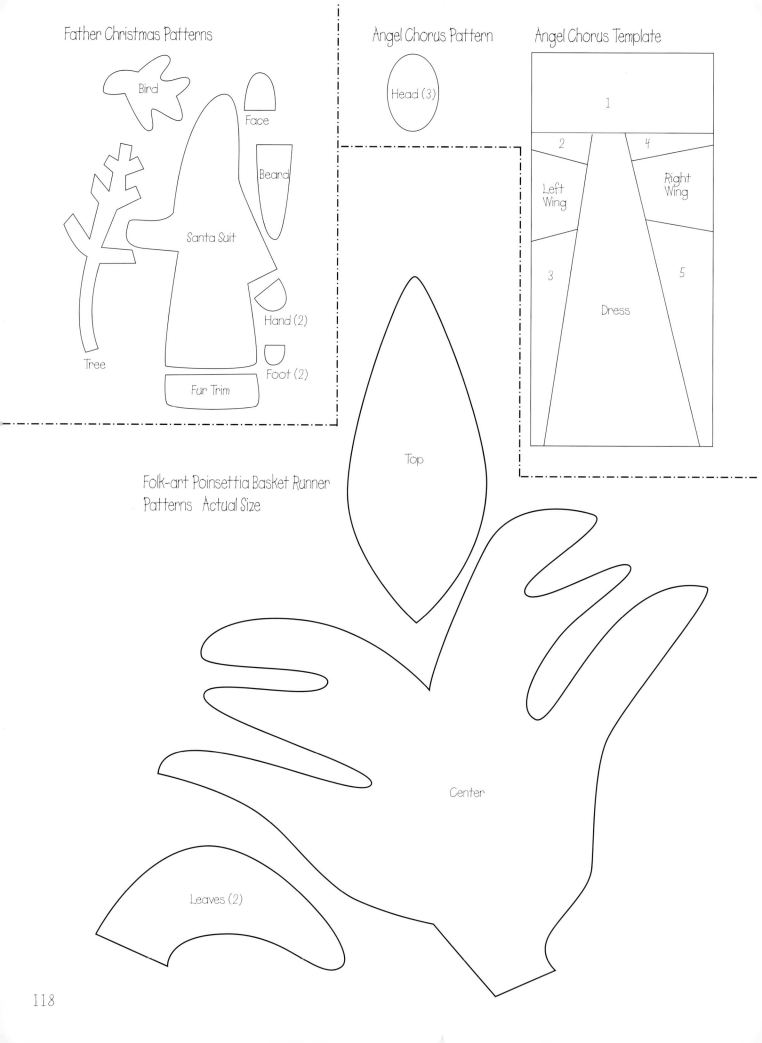

Father Christmas Patterns

Bird

Face

Beard

Santa Suit

Tree

Hand (2)

Foot (2)

Fur Trim

Angel Chorus Pattern

Head (3)

Angel Chorus Template

1

2

4

Left
Wing

Right
Wing

3

5

Dress

Folk-art Poinsettia Basket Runner
Patterns Actual Size

Top

Center

Leaves (2)

118

Snowcapped Tree Template

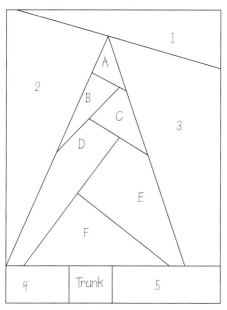

1

2

A

B

C

3

D

E

F

4 | Trunk | 5

Carolers Patterns

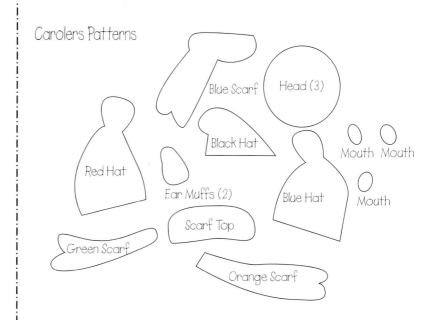

Blue Scarf

Head (3)

Black Hat

Red Hat

Mouth Mouth

Ear Muffs (2)

Blue Hat

Mouth

Scarf Top

Green Scarf

Orange Scarf

Antique Christmas Star Patterns

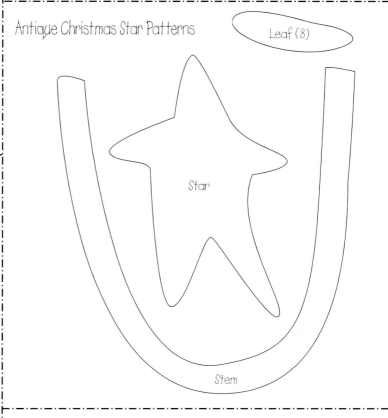

Leaf (8)

Star

Stem

Eight-point Star Template

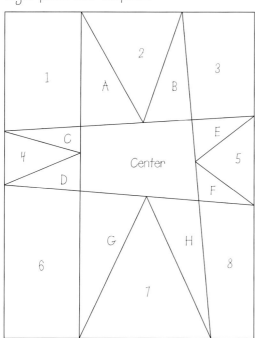

1

2

3

A

B

C

E

4

Center

5

D

F

G

H

6

7

8

Crazy-quilt Heart Template

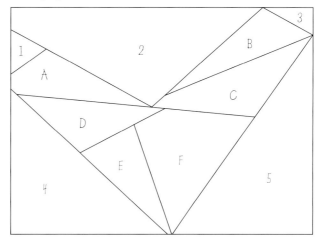

3

1

2

B

A

C

D

E

F

4

5

Folk-art Angel Patterns

Head

Star

Wing (2)

Hand (2)

Dress

Foot (2)

Cat Angel Template

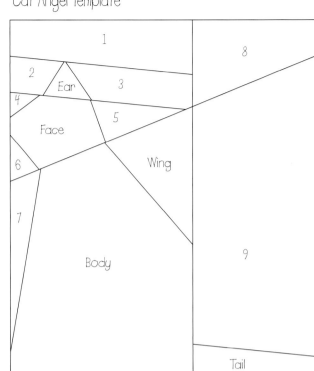

1

8

2

Ear

3

4

5

Face

Wing

6

7

Body

9

Tail

Cat Angel Patterns

Halo

Star

Angel with Garland Template

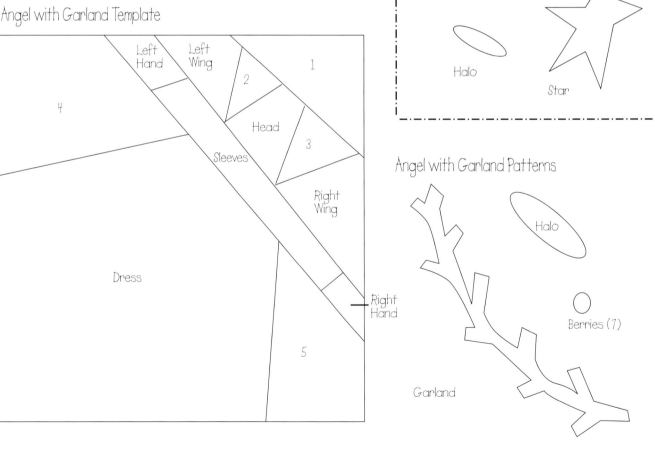

Left Hand

Left Wing

1

2

4

Head

3

Sleeves

Right Wing

Dress

Right Hand

5

Angel with Garland Patterns

Halo

Berries (7)

Garland

Angel with Harp Template

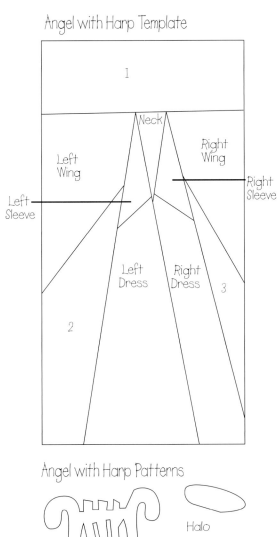

1

Neck

Left Wing

Right Wing

Left Sleeve

Right Sleeve

Left Dress

Right Dress

2

3

Angel with Harp Patterns

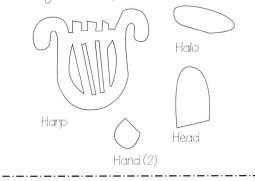

Halo

Harp

Head

Hand (2)

Dashing Through the Snow Patterns

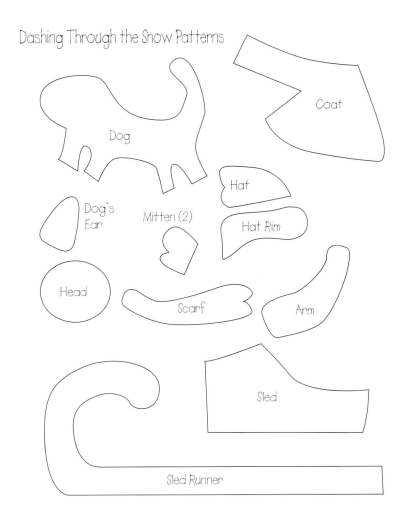

Dog

Coat

Hat

Dog's Ear

Mitten (2)

Hat Rim

Head

Scarf

Arm

Sled

Sled Runner

Chili Pepper Template

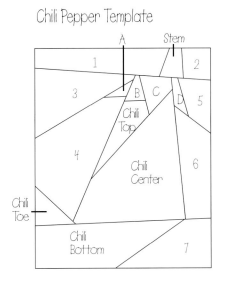

A

Stem

1

2

3

B

C

D

5

Chili Top

4

Chili Center

6

Chili Toe

Chili Bottom

7

Button Tree Patterns

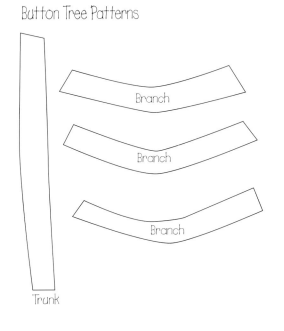

Branch

Branch

Branch

Trunk

Santa Claus Quilt Patterns Actual Size

Hat Ball

Glove

Hat Fur

Boot Fur

Heart

Arm

Head

Teddy Bear

Bow Tie

Foot Pad

Leg

Arm Pad

Muzzle

Foot Pad

Candy Cane (3)

Ornament (10)

Star

Medium Bow

Small Bow

Large Bow

Santa claus comes but once a year bringing presents and good cheer

Embroidery Placement

Alternative Verse

Santa claus, I want it all.

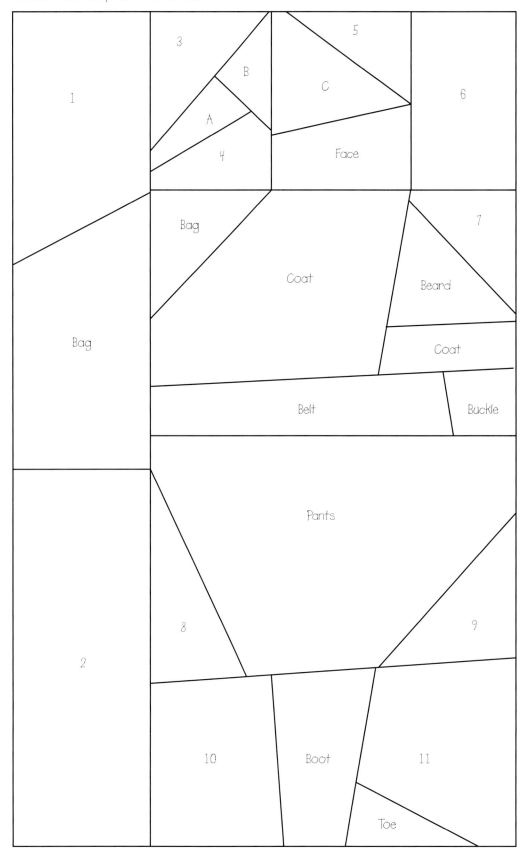

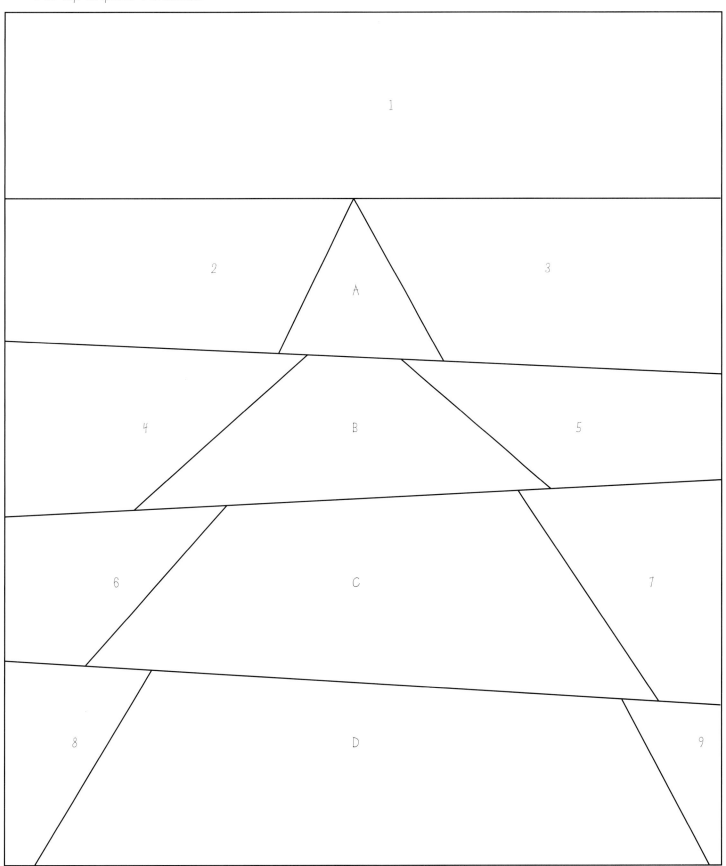

Tree Bottom Template Actual Size

10

11

E

12

15

16

18

Tree
Trunk

13

Left Present

14

17

Center Present

Right Present

Rose Poinsettia Template

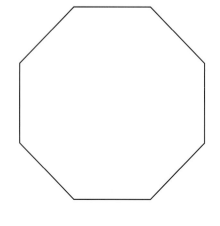

Star Garland Patterns Actual Size

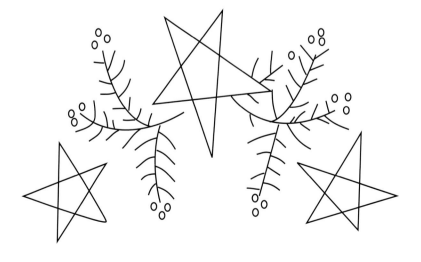

Down the Chimney Template

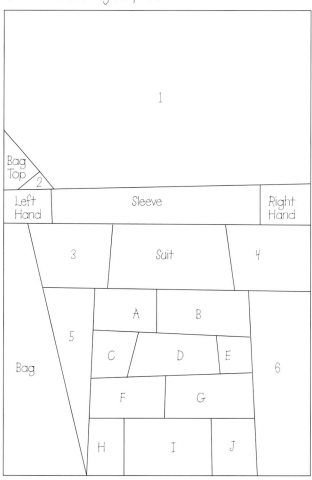

Down the Chimney Patterns

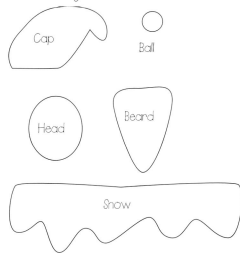

Cap

Ball

Head

Beard

Snow

Plum Pudding Template

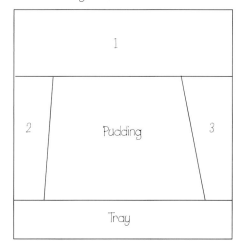

Plum Pudding Patterns

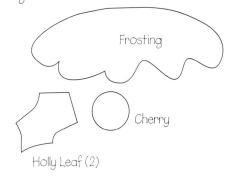

Frosting

Cherry

Holly Leaf (2)

Christmas Top Template

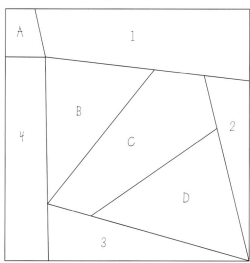

Ginger Baskets Patterns

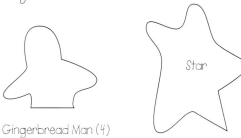

Star

Gingerbread Man (4)

Crazy-quilt Angel Template

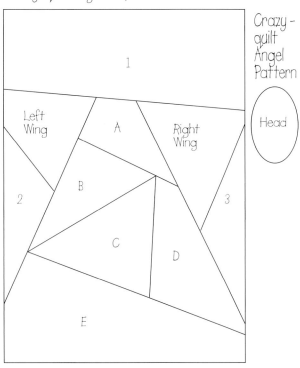

1

Left Wing   A   Right Wing

2   B

C   D

3

E

Crazy-quilt Angel Pattern

Head

Christmas Heart Template

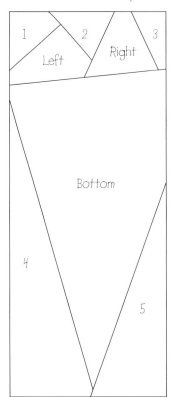

1   2   3

Left   Right

Bottom

4   5

Christmas Heart Patterns

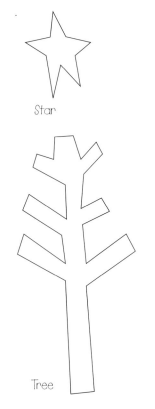

Star

Tree

Snowman with Broom Patterns

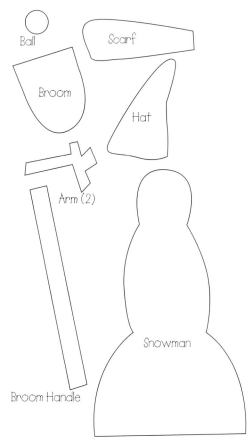

Ball

Scarf

Broom

Hat

Arm (2)

Snowman

Broom Handle

Snow Angel Patterns

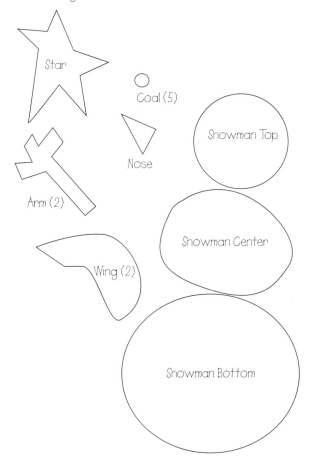

Star

Coal (5)

Nose

Arm (2)

Wing (2)

Snowman Top

Snowman Center

Snowman Bottom

Farmer Santa Template

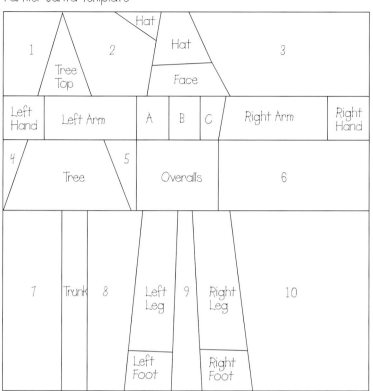

	Hat		
1	2	Hat	3
	Tree Top	Face	

Left Hand	Left Arm	A	B	C	Right Arm	Right Hand

4		5			
	Tree		Overalls	6	

7	Trunk	8	Left Leg	9	Right Leg	10
			Left Foot		Right Foot	

Farmer Santa Patterns

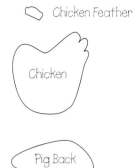

Chicken Feather

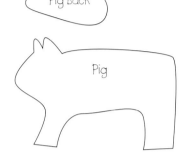

Chicken

Pig Back

Pig

Jolly Santa Patterns

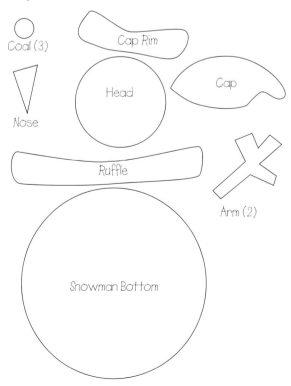

Coal (3)

Cap Rim

Nose

Head

Cap

Ruffle

Arm (2)

Snowman Bottom

Merry Christmas to Moo Patterns

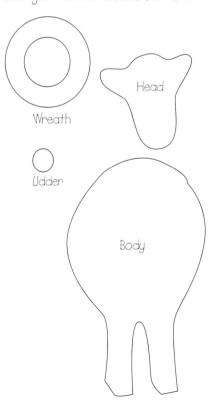

Wreath

Head

Udder

Body

129

Christmas Treats Template

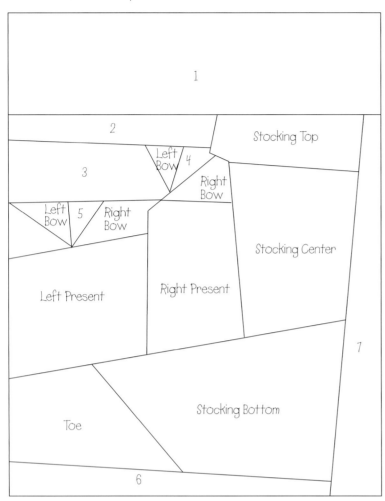

Christmas Treats Patterns

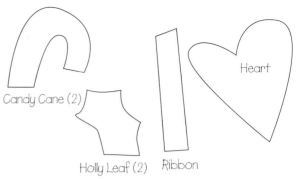

Candy Cane (2)

Holly Leaf (2) Ribbon Heart

Folk-art Reindeer Patterns

Antlers

Star

Reindeer

Star Flake Pattern

Star Flake

Reindeer Joy Patterns

Star Nose

Winter Garden Quilt Template   Actual Size

Arch Angel Patterns

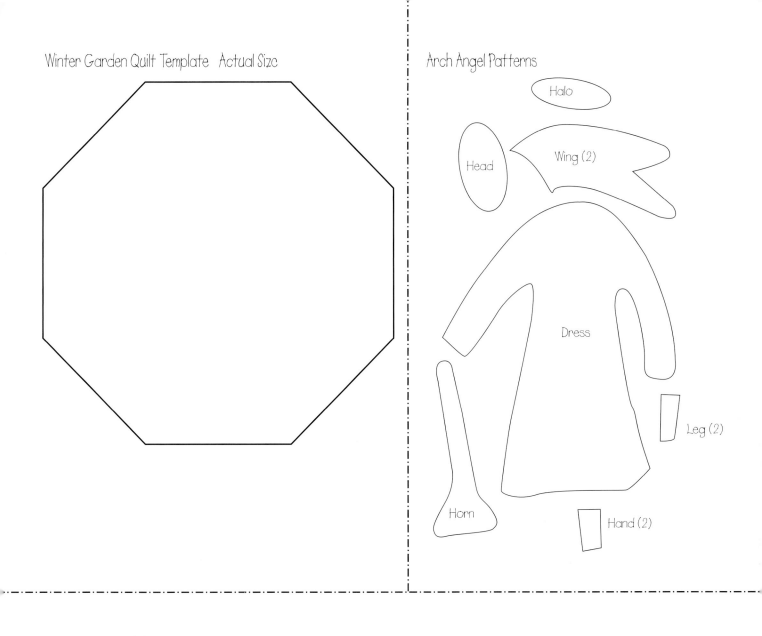

Halo

Head

Wing (2)

Dress

Leg (2)

Horn

Hand (2)

Forest Friends Patterns

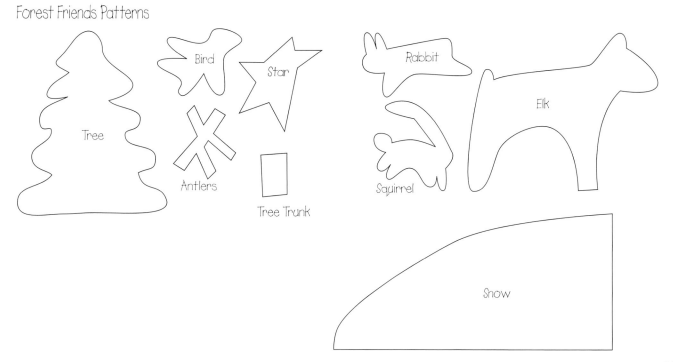

Tree

Bird

Star

Antlers

Tree Trunk

Rabbit

Elk

Squirrel

Snow

131

Santa in Sleigh Template

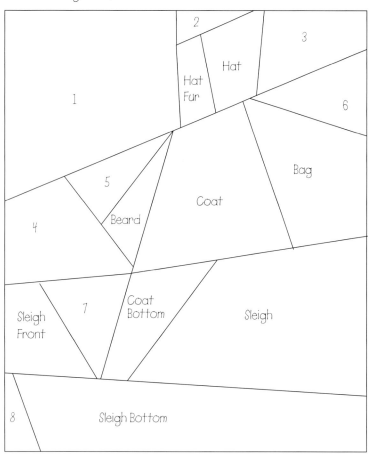

1

2

3

Hat

Hat
Fur

6

5

Bag

Beard

Coat

4

7

Coat
Bottom

Sleigh

Sleigh
Front

8

Sleigh Bottom

Santa in Sleigh Patterns

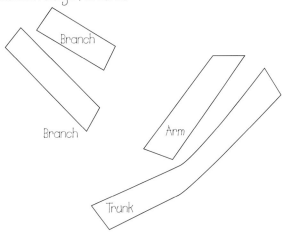

Branch

Branch

Arm

Trunk

Peace Sheep Patterns

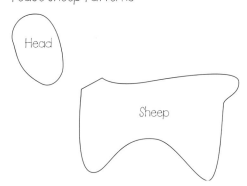

Head

Sheep

Frosty's House Template

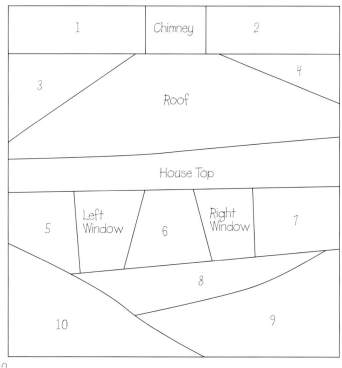

1

Chimney

2

3

4

Roof

House Top

5

Left
Window

6

Right
Window

7

8

10

9

Frosty's House Patterns

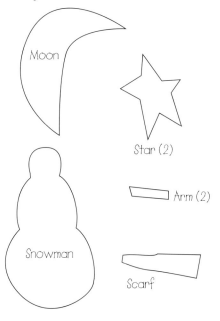

Moon

Star (2)

Arm (2)

Snowman

Scarf

Pieced Snowman Template

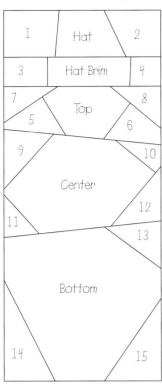

| 1 | Hat | 2 |

Hat Brim: 3, 4

Top: 7, 5, 8, 6

Center: 9, 10, 11, 12, 13

Bottom: 14, 15

Pinecone Template

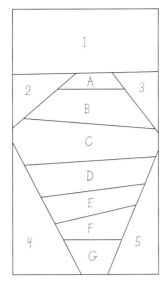

1

2, A, 3

B

C

D

E

F, 5

4, G

Pinecone Pattern

Branch

Pear Template

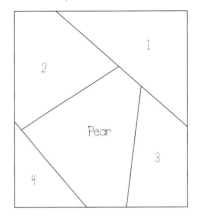

2, 1

Pear

3

4

Pear Pattern

Leaf (2)

Santa Claws Patterns

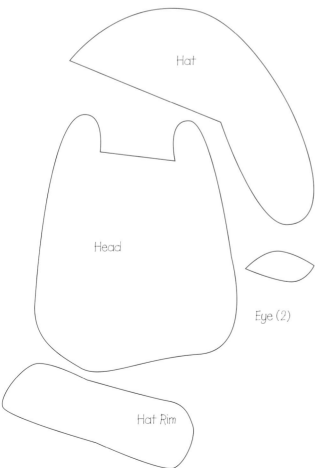

Hat

Head

Hat Rim

Eye (2)

Mitten Template

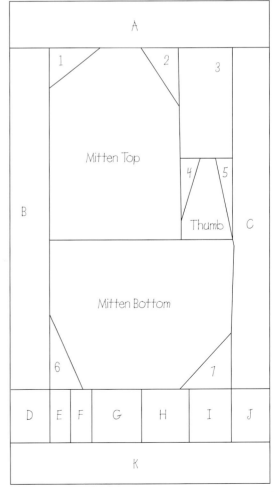

A

1, 2, 3

Mitten Top

4, 5

B, Thumb, C

Mitten Bottom

6, 7

| D | E | F | G | H | I | J |

K

Cardinal Template

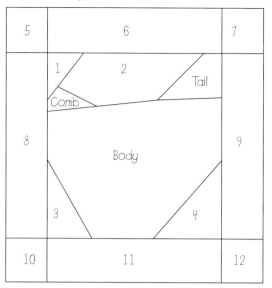

| 5 | 6 | 7 |

Beak

1 2 Tail
Comb

8 Body 9

3 4

| 10 | 11 | 12 |

Country Tree Template

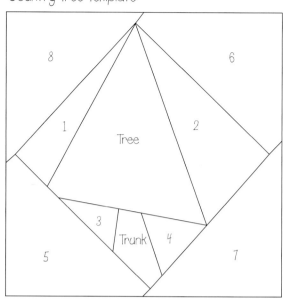

8 6

1 Tree 2

3 Trunk 4

5 7

Primitive Stocking Template

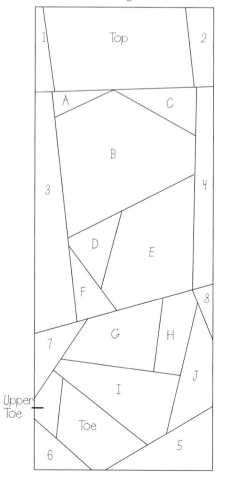

1 Top 2

A C

B

3 4

D E

F

8

7 G H

J

Upper
Toe

I

Toe

6 5

Cabin in the Woods Template

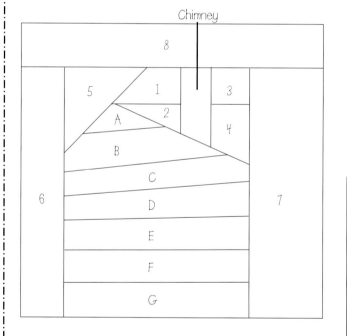

Chimney

8

5 1 3

A 2

4

B

6 C 7

D

E

F

G

Cabin in the Woods Patterns

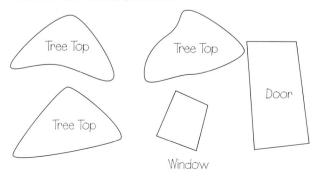

Tree Top

Tree Top

Tree Top

Door

Trunk

Trunk

Window

Christmas Farm Template

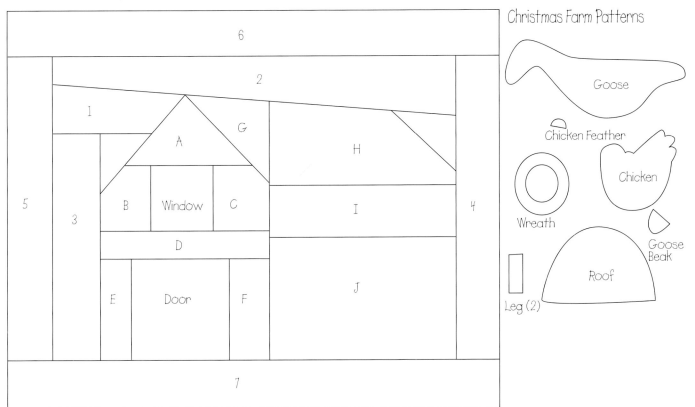

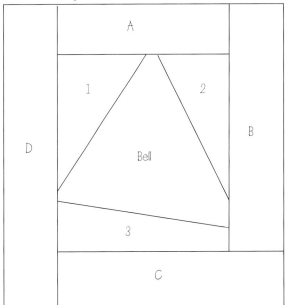

Christmas Farm Patterns

Goose

Chicken Feather

Chicken

Wreath

Goose Beak

Roof

Leg (2)

Heart & Mitten Patterns

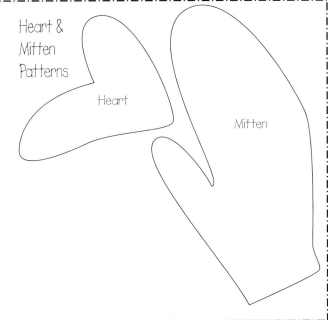

Heart

Mitten

Bell with Holly Template

A

1

2

B

D

Bell

3

C

Bell with Holly Patterns

Holly Leaf

Bell

Handle

Holly Berry Patterns

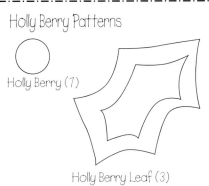

Holly Berry (7)

Holly Berry Leaf (3)

Choo Choo Train Template

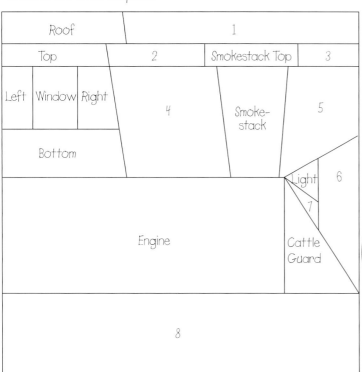

Roof			1	
Top		2	Smokestack Top	3
Left	Window	Right	4	Smoke-stack	5
Bottom					6

Light

Engine

7

Cattle Guard

8

Choo Choo Train Patterns

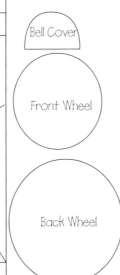

Bell Cover

Front Wheel

Back Wheel

Blue Santa Template

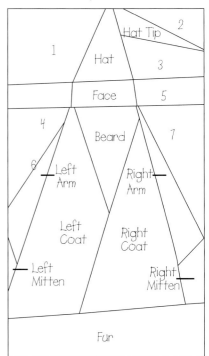

1	Hat	Hat Tip	2
		3	
Face		5	
4	Beard	7	

6 Left Arm   Right Arm

Left Coat   Right Coat

Left Mitten   Right Mitten

Fur

Nutcracker Template

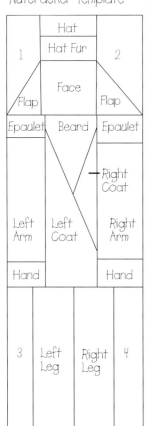

1	Hat	2
	Hat Fur	
Flap	Face	Flap
Epaulet	Beard	Epaulet
Left Arm	Left Coat	Right Coat
		Right Arm
Hand		Hand
3	Left Leg	Right Leg	4

Starflower Patterns

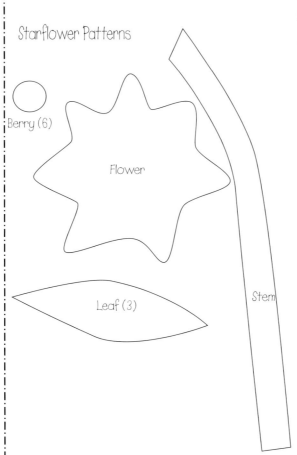

Berry (6)

Flower

Stem

Leaf (3)

Snowman with Stick Tree Patterns

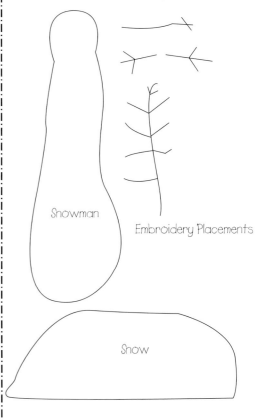

Snowman

Embroidery Placements

Snow

Christmas Crow Patterns

Crow

Hat

Hat Rim

Embroidery Patterns

Christmas Is Heavenly Patterns

Angel with Tree Template

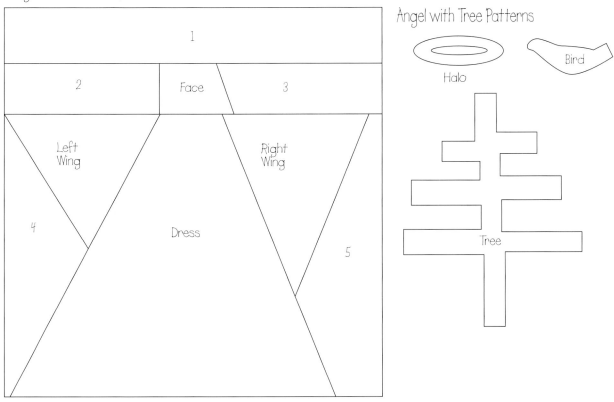

1

2

Face

3

Left
Wing

Right
Wing

4

Dress

5

Angel with Tree Patterns

Halo

Bird

Tree

Gold Santa Template

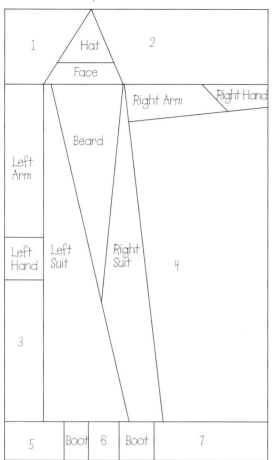

Candlelit Tree Template

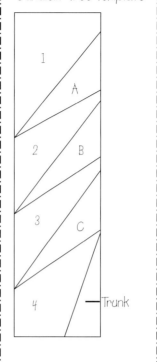

Primitive Candy Cane Template

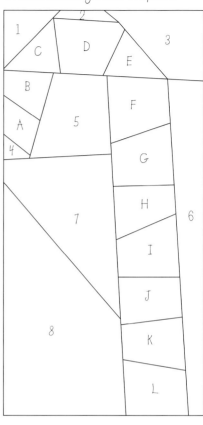

Reindeer with Holly Pattern

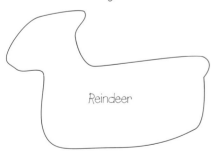

Angel with Star Template

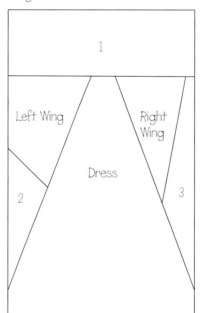

Angel with Star Patterns

Moose Pattern

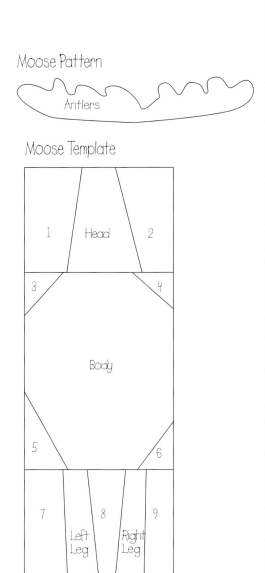

Antlers

Moose Template

1 | Head | 2

3 | 4

Body

5 | 6

7 | 8 | 9

Left Leg | Right Leg

Simple Angel Template

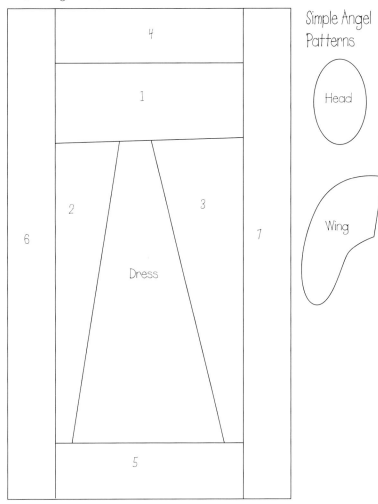

4

1

2 | 3

6 | 7

Dress

5

Simple Angel Patterns

Head

Wing

Red Bird with Star Template

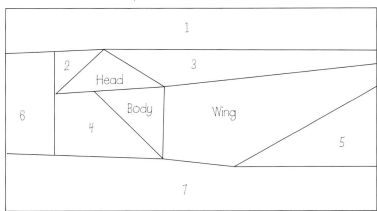

1

2 | 3

Head

6 | Body | Wing

4 | 5

7

Red Bird with Star Pattern

Star

139

Forever Love Template

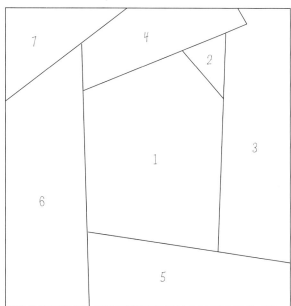

```
7          4
              2

     1            3
6

        5
```

Forever Love Patterns

Snowball with Heart Patterns

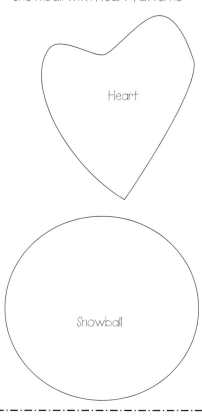

Heart

Snowball

Gingerbread House Template

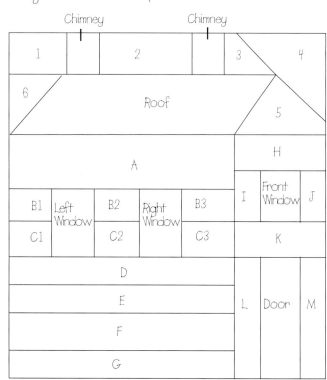

Chimney   Chimney

```
1      2      3    4
6        Roof
                  5
          A         H
B1  Left  B2  Right  B3   I  Front   J
    Window    Window          Window
C1    C2      C3         K
      D
      E         L  Door  M
      F
      G
```

Gingerbread House Patterns

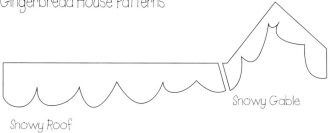

Snowy Roof   Snowy Gable

Tree in Cabin Template

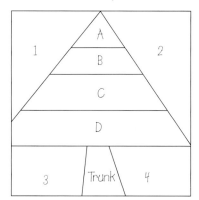

```
      A
1           2
      B
      C
      D
3   Trunk   4
```

140

Gold Star Template

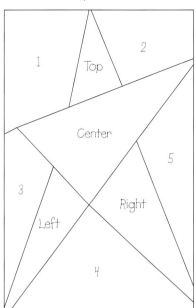

1
2
Top
Center
5
3
Right
Left
4

Baby Jesus Template

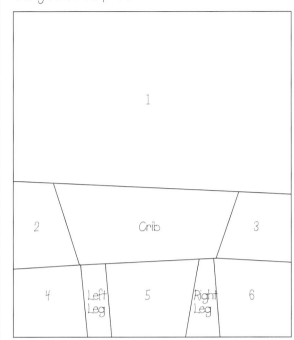

1

2
Crib
3

4
Left Leg
5
Right Leg
6

Baby Jesus Patterns

Swaddling Clothes

Star

Halo

Head

Littlest Angel Template

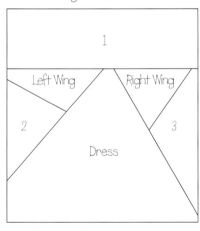

1

Left Wing
Right Wing

2
3
Dress

Littlest Angel Pattern

Head

Wool Snowflake Patterns

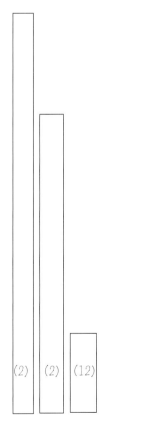

(2)
(2)
(12)

Christmas House Patterns

Trim

Bow (4)

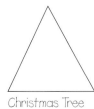

Christmas Tree

Wreath

141

Shepherd Template

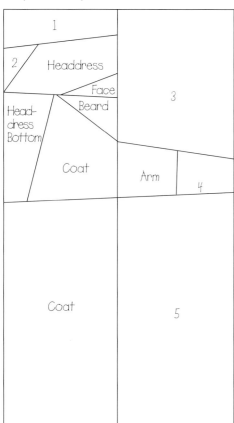

1

2

Headdress

Face

Beard

Head-
dress
Bottom

3

Coat

Arm

4

Coat

5

Candle Template

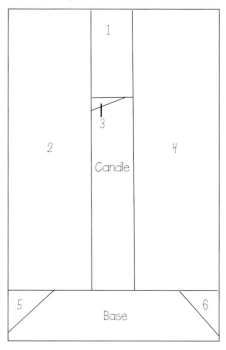

1

3

2

Candle

4

5

Base

6

Candle Patterns

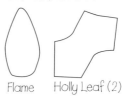

Flame

Holly Leaf (2)

Shepherd Patterns

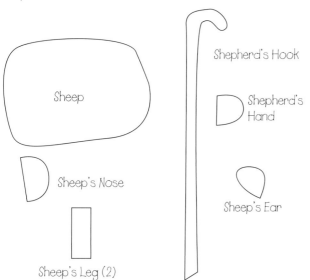

Sheep

Sheep's Nose

Sheep's Leg (2)

Shepherd's Hook

Shepherd's
Hand

Sheep's Ear

Dove with Berries Patterns

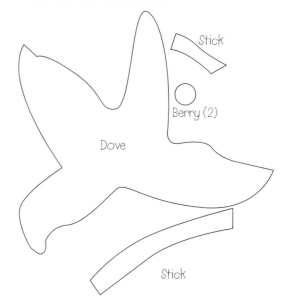

Stick

Berry (2)

Dove

Stick

Rejoice Template

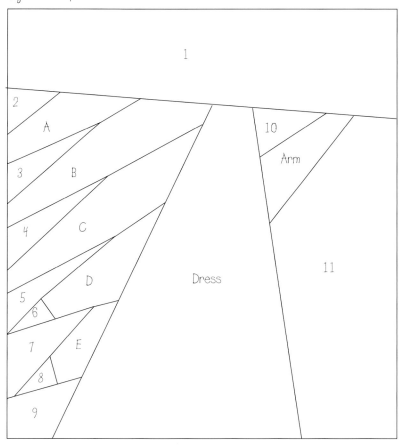

1

2

A

3

B

4

C

10

Arm

5

D

6

Dress

11

7

E

8

9

Rejoice Patterns

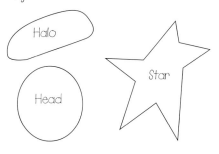

Halo

Head

Star

Christmas Flower Patterns

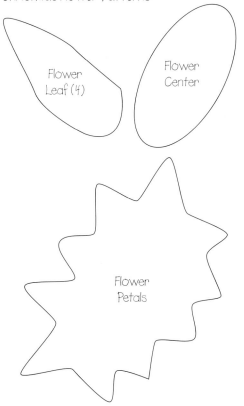

Flower Leaf (4)

Flower Center

Flower Petals

Noel Template

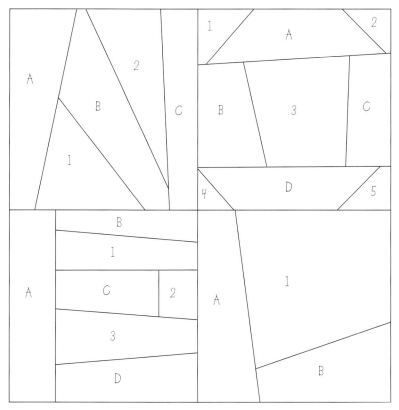

A

2

B

C

1

1

A

2

B

3

C

4

D

5

B

1

A

C

2

A

1

3

D

B

Scrap Heart Template

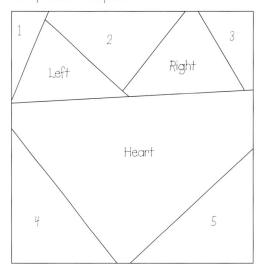

1

2

3

Left

Right

Heart

4

5

Christmas Town Template

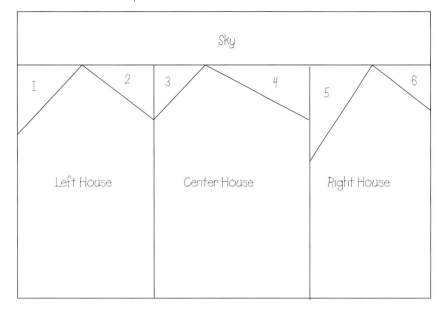

Christmas Town Patterns

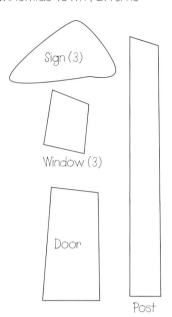

Dove Wreath Template

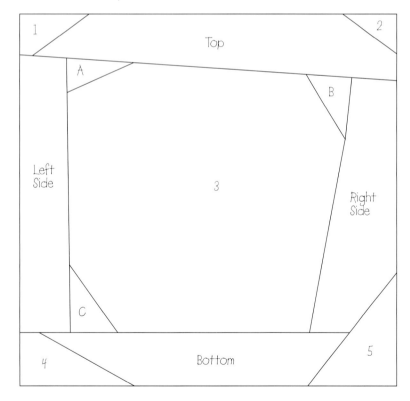

Dove Wreath Patterns

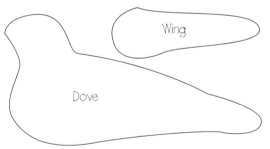

Heavenly Star Template

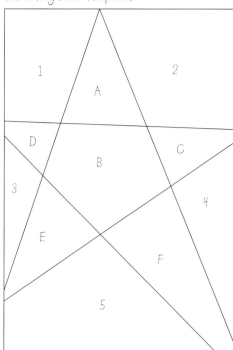

1   2

A

D   C

B

3   4

E

F

5

Folk-art Snowman Patterns

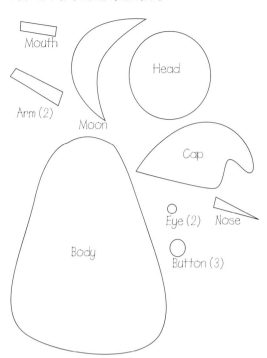

Mouth

Arm (2)

Moon

Head

Cap

Eye (2)

Nose

Body

Button (3)

Plump Angel Template

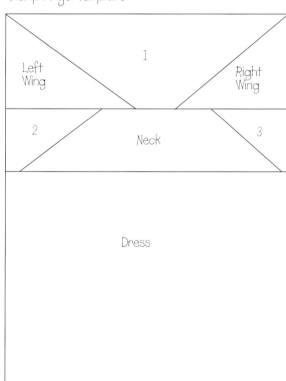

Left Wing

1

Right Wing

2   Neck   3

Dress

Plump Angel Patterns

Halo

Head

Holly Basket Patterns

Holly Berry (3)

Holly Berry Leaf (3)

Star Four Patch Template

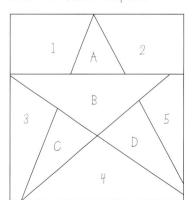

1   A   2

B

3   5

C   D

4

Christmas Cookies Patterns

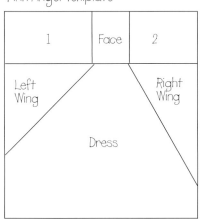

Glove

Gingerbread Man

Star

Tree

Church Template

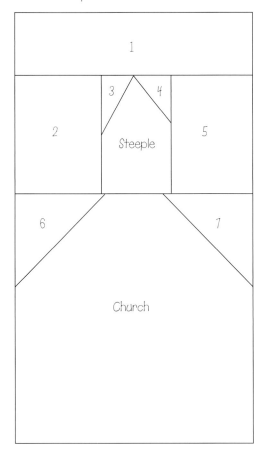

1

3   4

2   Steeple   5

6   7

Church

Pink Angel Template

1   Face   2

Left Wing   Right Wing

Dress

Church Patterns

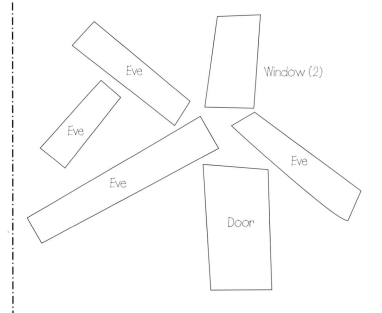

Eve

Eve

Eve

Eve

Window (2)

Eve

Door

Snowman Ornament Template

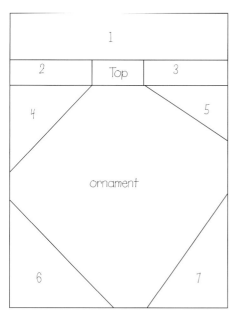

1		
2	Top	3

4

5

ornament

6

7

Snowman Ornament Pattern

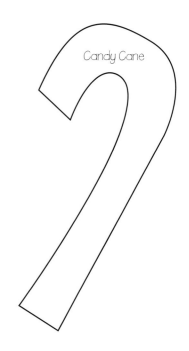

Candy Cane

Crazy Joy Quilt Patterns   Actual Size

Snowman

Star

Gingerbread Man

Wreath

147

Antique Santa Template

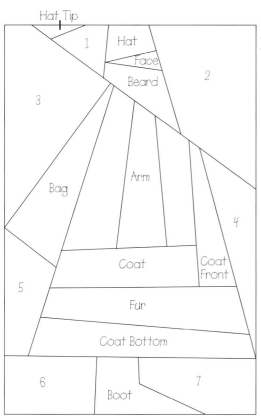

Hat Tip

1 Hat

Face

Beard

2

3

Bag

Arm

4

5

Coat   Coat Front

Fur

Coat Bottom

6   Boot   7

Antique Santa Pattern

Glove

Folk-art Star Patterns

Left

Top

Center

Right

Left Bottom

Right Bottom

Meowy Christmas Patterns

Plain Santa Patterns

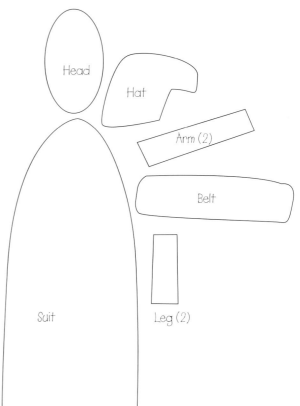

Head

Hat

Arm (2)

Belt

Suit

Leg (2)

Toy Drum Template

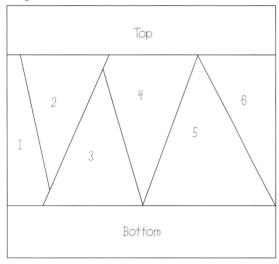

Top

2
4
6
1
3
5

Bottom

Holiday Bell Template

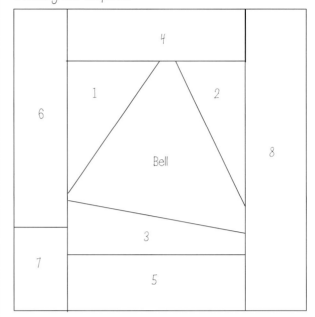

4
1
6
2
Bell
8
7
3
5

Holiday Bell Patterns

Handle

Clacker

Basket with Holly Template

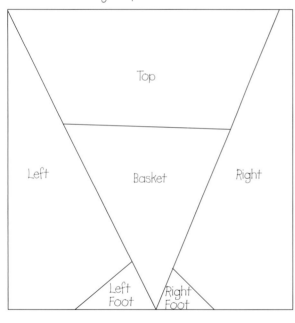

Top

Left
Basket
Right

Left Foot
Right Foot

Fruit Basket Patterns

Leaf

Pear

Reindeer Face Template

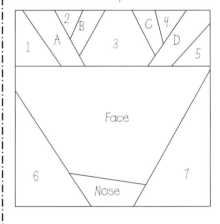

1
A
2
B
3
C
4
D
5
Face
6
Nose
7

Basket with Holly Patterns

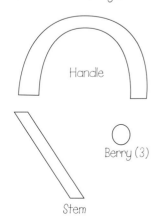

Handle

Berry (3)

Stem

Crazy Candy Cane Template

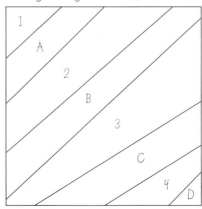

1
A
2
B
3
C
4
D

Christmas Hand & Heart Patterns

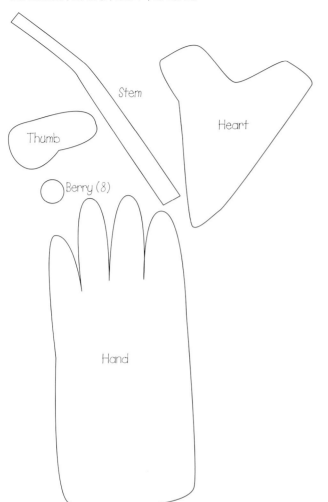

Stem

Heart

Thumb

Berry (8)

Hand

Pieced Pineapple Template

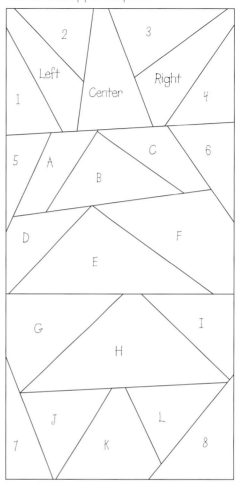

Poinsettia Basket Template

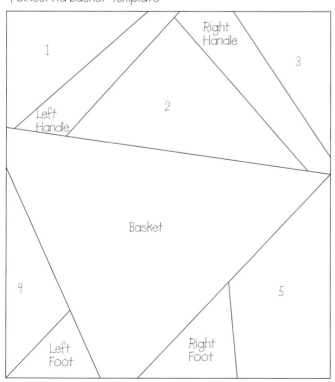

Poinsettia Basket Patterns

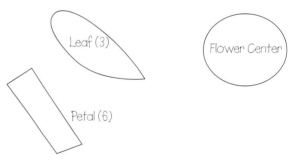

Leaf (3)

Flower Center

Petal (6)

Joy Wreath Patterns

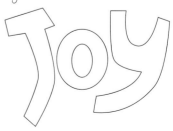

Pear Tree Template

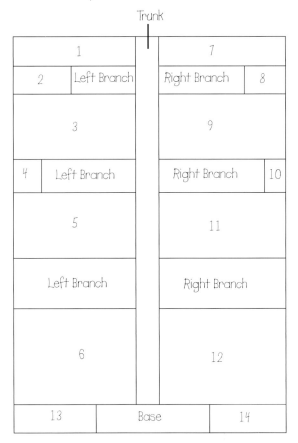

Trunk

1			7	
2	Left Branch		Right Branch	8
3			9	
4	Left Branch		Right Branch	10
5			11	
Left Branch			Right Branch	
6			12	
13		Base		14

Pear Tree Patterns

Star

Heart

Pear

Bird

Snowbunny Patterns

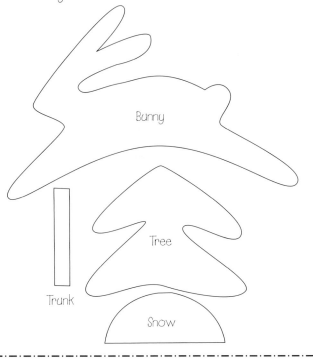

Bunny

Tree

Trunk

Snow

Jingle Bells Patterns

Bell (3)

jingle bells

Embroidery Patterns

Little Santa Template

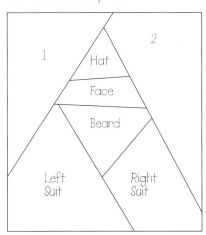

1

2

Hat

Face

Beard

Left Suit

Right Suit

Star Ornament Template

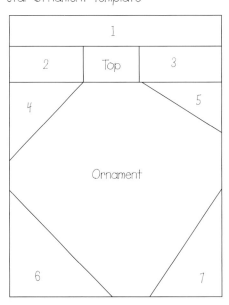

1		
2	Top	3
4		5
	Ornament	
6		7

Star Ornament Pattern

Star

Rocking Horse Template

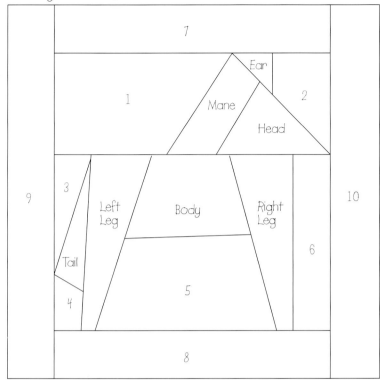

Rocking Horse Patterns

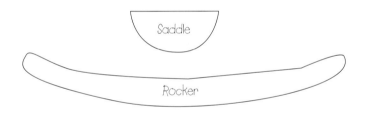

Saddle

Rocker

Mistletoe Patterns

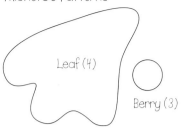

Leaf (4)

Berry (3)

Stocking Template

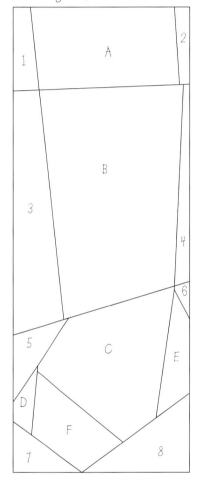

Mistletoe Wreath Patterns

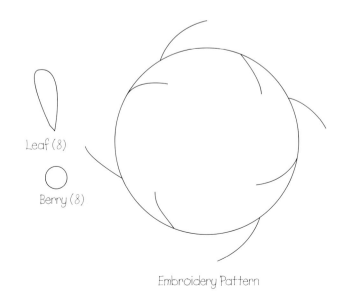

Leaf (8)

Berry (8)

Embroidery Pattern

Gingerbread Man Pattern

Gingerbread Man

St. Nick with Tree Template

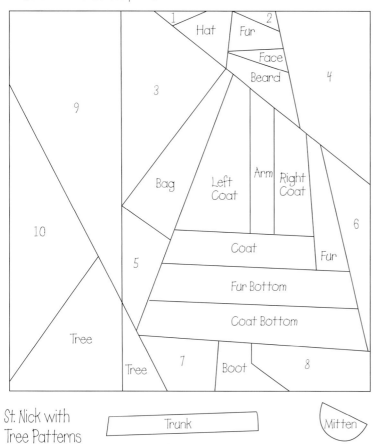

St. Nick with
Tree Patterns

Snowman with Boots Patterns

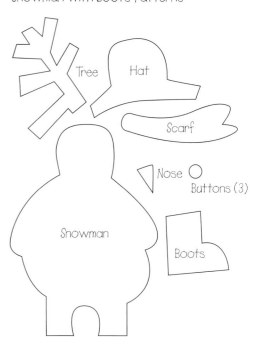

Holly Heart Template

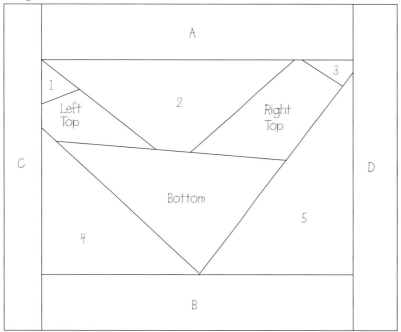

Holly Heart Pattern

Roly-poly Snowman Patterns

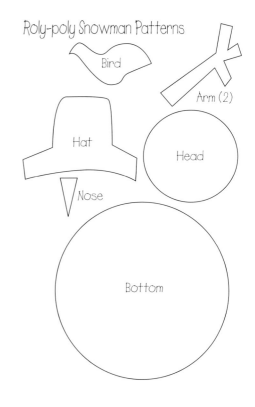

Winter Cabin Patterns

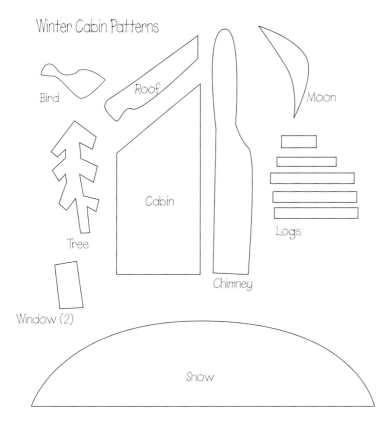

Bird

Roof

Moon

Tree

Cabin

Logs

Window (2)

Chimney

Snow

Cranberry Basket Patterns

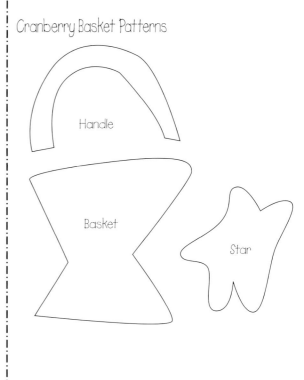

Handle

Basket

Star

Snowman Block Patterns

Arm (2)

Snowman

Christmas Angel Block Patterns

Halo

Head

Wings

Stocking Block Patterns

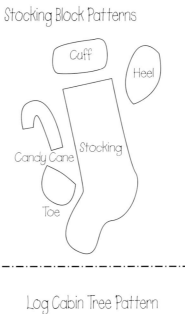

Cuff

Heel

Candy Cane

Stocking

Toe

Log Cabin Tree Pattern

Trunk

Feather Tree Pattern

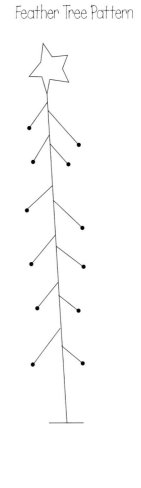

Liberty Angel Template

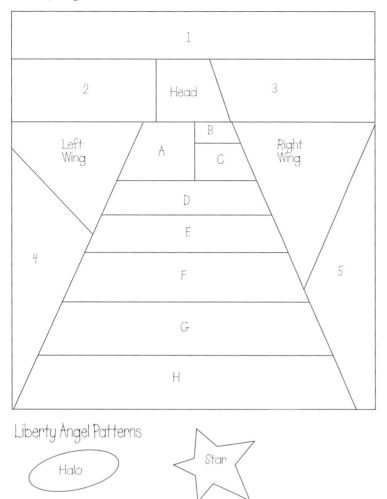

Liberty Angel Patterns

Halo

Star

Christmas Pine Tree Template

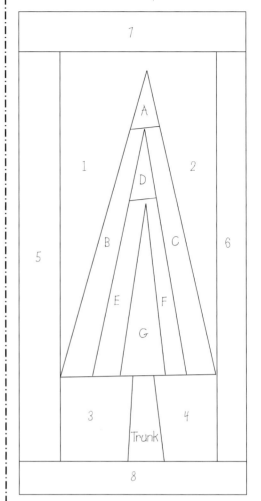

Christmas Pine Tree Pattern

Top

Tumbling Santa Template

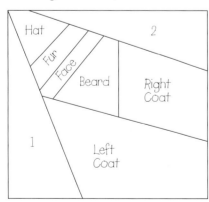

Spinning Trees Template

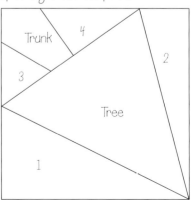

Plump Santa Template

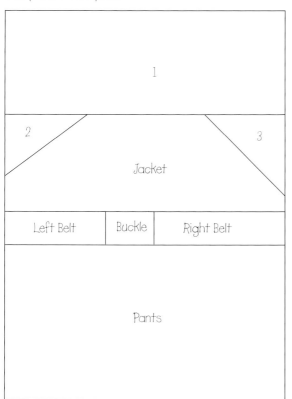

1		
2	Jacket	3
Left Belt	Buckle	Right Belt
	Pants	

Plump Santa Patterns

Hat

Head

Twisting Star Template

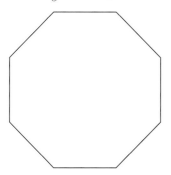

St. Nick Template

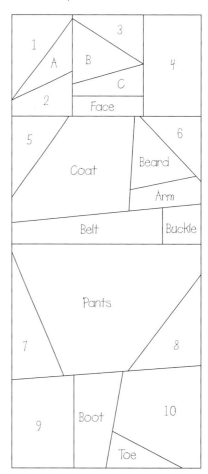

1 A B 3 4
2 C Face
5 Coat Beard 6
Arm
Belt Buckle
Pants
7 8
9 Boot 10
Toe

Crazy-strip Wreath Template

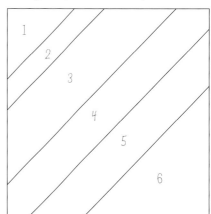

1
2
3
4
5
6

Plain Snowman Patterns

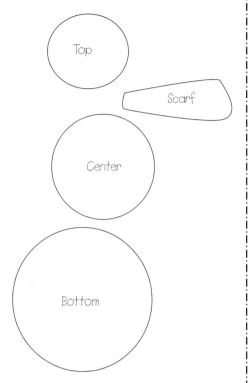

Top

Scarf

Center

Bottom

Frosty Patterns

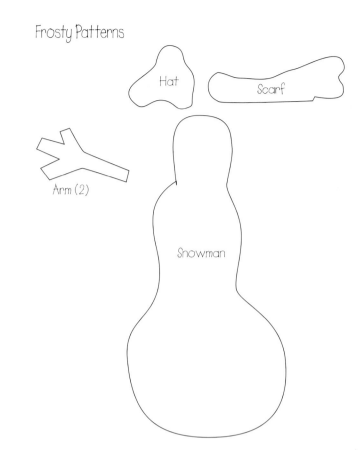

Hat

Scarf

Arm (2)

Snowman

Flying Angel Template

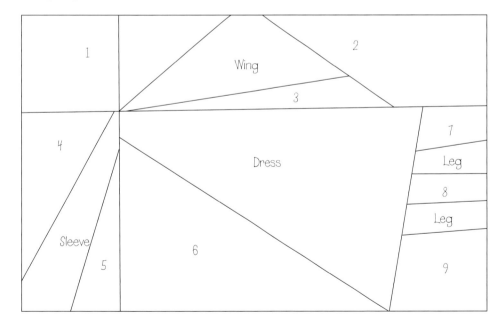

1

2

Wing

3

4

7

Leg

Dress

8

Leg

Sleeve

5

6

9

Flying Angel Pattern

Head

Wool Tree Patterns

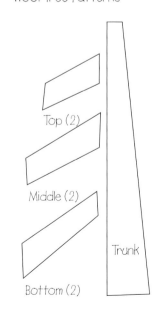

Top (2)

Middle (2)

Bottom (2)

Trunk

About the Author

Cheri Saffiote has been creative and artistic since she was a small child selling her watercolors at local craft fairs. In 1990, while raising her four children, she turned her attention to designing and teaching tole painting and quilting. She then went on to own a quilt store, Calico Station, in San Marcos, California, for eleven years. Cheri has self-published several quilting books, but now designs patterns and books for Indygo Junction and Chapelle, Limited. She continues to teach quilting classes in the Southern California area. When she is not quilting, she is outside gardening. She and her new husband Greg live in Poway, California, with their many cats, chickens, and dogs.

Christmas has always been a very inspirational time of year for Cheri. There are so many traditional and folk-art ideas—snowmen, trees, and angels, just to name a few. One of Cheri's greatest pleasures is to make holiday quilts for her family and friends. With all the many holiday designs in *301 Country Christmas Blocks*, you, too, can create some wonderful quilt projects for your family and friends. Stitch away, stitch away, stitch away, all! Happy Holidays.

Metric Conversion Chart

mm-millimetres   cm-centimetres
inches to millimetres and centimetres

inches	mm	cm	inches	cm	inches	cm
1/8	3	0.3	9	22.9	30	76.2
1/4	6	0.6	10	25.4	31	78.7
3/8	10	1.0	11	27.9	32	81.3
1/2	13	1.3	12	30.5	33	83.8
5/8	16	1.6	13	33.0	34	86.4
3/4	19	1.9	14	35.6	35	88.9
7/8	22	2.2	15	38.1	36	91.4
1	25	2.5	16	40.6	37	94.0
1 1/4	32	3.2	17	43.2	38	96.5
1 1/2	38	3.8	18	45.7	39	99.1
1 3/4	44	4.4	19	48.3	40	101.6
2	51	5.1	20	50.8	41	104.1
2 1/2	64	6.4	21	53.3	42	106.7
3	76	7.6	22	55.9	43	109.2
3 1/2	89	8.9	23	58.4	44	111.8
4	102	10.2	24	61.0	45	114.3
4 1/2	114	11.4	25	63.5	46	116.8
5	127	12.7	26	66.0	47	119.4
6	152	15.2	27	68.6	48	121.9
7	178	17.8	28	71.1	49	124.5
8	203	20.3	29	73.7	50	127.0

Index